"This book is a valuable yearlong calendar of the life of the fourteen Cistercian nuns of the Mariakloster on Tautra Island in the Trondheim Fjord of Norway. Their extraordinary relationship to the natural world around them is compellingly described by four of them who are gifted writers and poets. Looking at nature broadly through the lens of their religious practice, they also examine their faith and commitment intimately through the lens of nature. The experiences of seasonal and temporal variations of darkness and light in the fjord are especially important to the deepening of their faith practice and their ever-growing connection to the spiritual world."

> — Robert Benson, PhD
> Professor Emeritus
> Miami University
> Oxford, Ohio

MONASTIC WISDOM SERIES: NUMBER SIXTY

Northern Light

The Cistercian Nuns of Tautra Mariakloster

Preface by
Dom Brendan Freeman, OCSO

α

Cistercian Publications
www.cistercianpublications.org

LITURGICAL PRESS
Collegeville, Minnesota
www.litpress.org

A Cistercian Publications title published by Liturgical Press

Cistercian Publications
Editorial Offices
161 Grosvenor Street
Athens, Ohio 45701
www.cistercianpublications.org

Cover design by Ann Blattner.
Cover photo: This is not the aurora borealis but "perlemor skyer," "mother-of-pearl clouds," which is a different phenomenon. They are formed in the stratosphere at heights of 15,000 to 30,000 meters (9–18 miles) and temperatures under –78° C. Since these clouds are formed so high, the sun can shine on them from below the horizon. The sun's rays are broken in the ice crystals in the same way as in a prism, and the pastel colors appear.

Scripture quotations are from the Catholic Edition of the Revised Standard Version of the Bible and the New Revised Standard Version Bible: Catholic Edition. Catholic Edition of the Revised Standard Version of the Bible copyright © 1965, 1966 National Council of the Churches of Christ in the United States of America. Used by permission. All rights reserved worldwide. New Revised Standard Version Bible: Catholic Edition © 1989, 1993 National Council of the Churches of Christ in the United States of America. Used by permission. All rights reserved worldwide.

Scripture quotations are from liturgical texts used at Tautra Mariakloster.

Excerpts from the English translation of *The Roman Missal* © 2010, International Commission on English in the Liturgy Corporation. All rights reserved.

1   2   3   4   5   6   7   8   9

Library of Congress Cataloging-in-Publication Data

Title: Northern light / the Cistercian nuns of Tautra Mariakloster ; preface by Dom Brendan Freeman, OCSO.
Description: Collegeville, Minnesota : Cistercian Publications, Liturgical Press, 2020. | Series: Monastic wisdom series ; number sixty | Summary: "Four Cistercian nuns write of their experiences as monastics living close to the land, sky, and water on the island of Tautra in Norway following the liturgical year of the monastery while experiencing the changing seasons and landscape that help to shape their life of faith and light"—Provided by publisher.
Identifiers: LCCN 2020014186 (print) | LCCN 2020014187 (ebook) | ISBN 9780879071608 (paperback) | ISBN 9780879074609 (epub) | ISBN 9780879074609 (mobi) | ISBN 9780879074609 (pdf)
Subjects: LCSH: Cistercian nuns—Norway. | Monastic and religious life of women—Norway. | Tautra Mariakloster.
Classification: LCC BX4538.Z6 T38 2020 (print) | LCC BX4538.Z6 (ebook) | DDC 271/.97—dc23
LC record available at https://lccn.loc.gov/2020014186
LC ebook record available at https://lccn.loc.gov/2020014187

Table of Contents

Abbreviations

AASS	Acta Sanctorum, Société des Bollandistes
CF	Cistercian Fathers series
Const	Constitutions of the Cistercian Order of the Strict Observance
CSEL	Corpus Christianorum, series Latina
RB	*Regula Benedicti; Rule of Saint Benedict*
SBOp	Sancti Bernardi Opera, ed. Jean Leclercq, Henri Rochais, and C. H. Talbot
SC	Sermons on the Song of Songs, Bernard of Clairvaux

Preface

And indeed, which of you here, intending to build a tower,
would not first sit down and work out the cost to see if you
had enough to complete it? (Luke 14:28)

In the late 1990s this is exactly what the community of Our
Lady of the Mississippi Abbey did, sitting down together and
discussing the possibility of establishing a new community—in
monastic terms, "making a foundation"—and counting the
cost.

A prudent person setting out to build a house plans every
step of the way and thus forestalls disaster when unforeseen
expenses stop the project. However, building a house and starting a new community are very different things. The major
difference is that there is no way to determine beforehand
whether the new community will flourish or wither. Vocations
are the great unknown. Usually the place chosen is close to a
large Catholic population from which to draw vocations. So
when the sisters chose to send seven of their own to Norway
everyone wondered where the vocations would come from:
Norway is 2.9 percent Catholic. Be that as it may, off they went
in 1999.

Geoffrey Chaucer once said that from old fields comes new
corn. In our case the old fields are the well-established monasteries with an excess of members, making it time to plant
seeds in other territories. New foundations have notoriously
difficult beginnings. Even coming from well-established monasteries with a good source of income and a supply of vocations,
the newcomers still have to slowly organize a building project,
start an industry, and attract vocations. In 1964, for example,

Mount St. Mary's Abbey in Wrentham, Massachusetts, sent twelve sisters to establish a new community on the bluffs of the Mississippi River in Iowa. The immediate task of the new foundation, Our Lady of the Mississippi Abbey, was to convert a private home into a monastery. So they began by placing their chapel in the living room, their dormitory in the attic, and their refectory in the den. These were only temporary arrangements, but sometimes it takes a good few years before a proper monastery, with cloister and all the necessary rooms, is in place.

In Norway, Tautra Mariakloster—a daughter house of Our Lady of the Mississippi—was no different. The seven foundresses had to convert three small houses into monastic dwellings. Even though these homes were close together, everyone had to go outside several times a day, rain or shine, to move from the chapel to the refectory to the work areas and from there to the sleeping rooms. But what seems from a distance like a hardship was, as Sr. Hanne-Maria recalls it, a time to commune with nature while moving among the buildings (page 4).

On a cold March day, the 25th, to be exact, in 1999, the seven founding sisters, along with Mother Gail Fitzpatrick, the abbess of the founding house; Bishop Georg Müller of the diocese of Trondheim; friends of the monastery; and I, the father immediate of Mississippi Abbey and representing New Melleray Abbey in Iowa, assembled in a large tent for the first Mass of the foundation. After Mass we gathered outside by the bell tower, where the Cistercian Bishop Emeritus of Oslo, John Willem Gran, would bless the bells. It was a blustery day, but the sky was pure blue, and the distant mountains, accenting the blue with dazzling white snow, reflected in the fjord, only yards from where we stood. I said to myself, this is a cathedral, a cathedral of nature. The fjord became an essential part of the community, one of the sisters as it were, a companion that will never leave them and that joins them in praising and singing to God, and reflecting, just as the life of the sisters does, the beauty of God.

The book you are about to read will explain just how the place—this wonderful Trondheim Fjord, the mountains, and the sky—have become part of the community's identity. It is all woven into the thoughts of the sisters, even into their hearts and souls, and has become a locus of prayer. One could call it the liturgy of nature, particular to Tautra, celebrated alongside or even within all the liturgical celebrations that form the essence of the monastic life.

The desert fathers spoke of three liturgies: the liturgy of heaven, the liturgy on earth, reflecting the heavenly one, and the liturgy of the heart. After the desert hermits came together for a very simple recitation of psalms, they then returned to their cells to continue with the liturgy of the heart, the silent prayer of the heart that is continually at prayer. Would it be presumptuous to add a fourth—the liturgy of nature? I leave that to your judgment after you read and reflect on this book.

This is a remarkable book, comprising as it does three essays from each of four sisters of Tautra Mariakloster as they journey through one calendar year. Their words invite you into the inner life of their minds and hearts. It is a wonderful way to get a vivid inside view of how a monastery works and how monastics think. This book has life.

I remember once being in Chicago, going to the Art Institute, and walking through the various rooms until I came to the room of the Dutch Masters. Underneath each painting, resting on the floor and leaning against the wall, was a replica, evidently painted by senior students from the Institute's School of Art. The students were very good, and to my untrained eye they seemed to match the masterpieces very well. I studied them carefully, and as I did I saw the great difference between a student and a master. The masters' paintings had life in the faces. While the students' paintings could replicate almost every other facet of the paintings, they could not copy that elusive thing called life. How do you paint a face with life in it and not just an accurate portrait but no life?

These essays have life. As you read, you can feel it pulsing in the words to such an extent that you realize that there is more than just a good description of the flora and fauna of Tautra Island here; there is also a spiritual dimension, as if the veil to the other world is lifted ever so slightly. These sisters are sharing their contemplative vision with us. At first it appears to be a very ordinary account of everyday life in a Trappistine Monastery, but as you read, something begins to call to you from the unseen world. Thomas Merton has defined contemplation as the sudden awareness of the truth within the truth. In this book the sisters give wonderful descriptions of the cycles of nature and of monastic prayer, accurate and true—but there is a deeper truth in their words.

These essays are all the more authentic because the sisters did not set out to try to be spiritual. To my mind that would be an affectation. They simply set out to share with the reader their everyday life, and in so doing they revealed the hidden treasures of the inner life, always present but seldom experienced.

What the sisters are engaged in is not some esoteric or exotic mysticism; it simply reveals the depth of soul present in everyone, and yet hidden. Saint Paul tells us that we have died with Christ, and our life now is hidden in God; when Christ, who is your life, appears, you also will appear with him in glory (Col 3:3-4). Our true self has yet to appear in glory, but it appears in its human form even now when we receive life as a gift and listen with the ears of our heart to the call of being present everywhere in the world—if only we are silent enough to hear it.

This book also speaks to the many young and not so young people who are becoming more and more aware of the environment and our responsibility to care for it, our common home, in the famous words of Pope Francis. This is a new dimension of the spiritual life. Twenty-five years ago all of spiritual literature contained no mention of care for our common home; it is also not in the tradition. It arises as a result of concern that humans are a major cause of the climate change that more and more shows the results of wasteful living. We are all involved in what happens to our common home under the stars, and of the need to reverse the downward trend. This concern has the potential of uniting, perhaps for the first time, all facets of society—religious, political, commercial, and educational. Will this be the crisis that forces us to put our differences aside and work together to save our planet? If so, it will prove to be of the Spirit, and not only from human concern, good as that is. These essays are a window into the future of an environmental spirituality without the self-consciousness that would identify it with a movement or a political statement. It is just something that grew out of listening hearts attuned to the signs of the time.

The sisters of Tautra usually live in silence. They were invited by the editor of Cistercian Publications to share their experiences in living the contemplative community life. I like to think that the silent monastic life is reflected in the words of the Psalmist: "No speech, no words, no voice is heard, yet their span extends throughout the earth, their words to the utmost bounds of the world" (Ps 19:4-5).

This book shows what can happen when women dedicated to the contemplative monastic life let their hearts speak in words we can understand. There is no hidden agenda here, no propaganda or persuasion. It is the type of speaking the first disciples of Jesus remarked on when they said to him, "Now you are speaking plainly and not in veiled language" (John 16:29).

If we receive the message in the spirit in which it was given, we too can join the sisters in thanking God for the wonder of our being, for the wonder of all God's creation (Ps 139:14).

Dom Brendan Freeman, OCSO
Mellifont Abbey, Ireland

Light

which left the Pleiades
2000 years ago
arrived just when
a Mayan's eye
peered upwards
through the stone shaft
of the Temple of the Jaguar Sun.

Other rays

began their earthward journey
before I even existed
to meet my eye
in the expanse of arctic sky
after Vigils.

Grace

sets out from God
before I need it
rushes light-years toward me
meets me the very moment I fall.

When it arrives
I am there.

Sr. Sheryl Frances Chen, OCSO

The Gift of Beauty

Sr. Hanne-Maria Berentzen, OCSO

O Lord, open my lips, and my mouth shall declare your praise.

The first words of a New Year, 4:20 in the morning, repeated three times. The first words of each day of the year. The opening verse of the Night Office is forming us in the life of Christ: *First of all, when you start a good work,* says Saint Benedict in his monastic rule, *you must beg him for his help.* With God's help I can open my mouth to do what is the deepest meaning of life: Singing his praise. Every New Year's first day, every new day, we deeply touch the meaning of our existence. Then we enter the theme of this special day as we sing,

> *Come, let us celebrate the Virgin Mary, the Mother of God! Let us adore her Son, Christ our Lord!*

On the Octave day of Christmas our celebration of the incarnation focuses on Mary, the Mother of God. Singing the Office of the Hours seven times a day, the Word of God sings its way into our hearts, and from the heart it returns to the mind, forming our whole being. Our life is a life of song. The antiphons enveloping each psalm stay in mind and body through the melody. This first day of a New Year, entered in winter darkness as in the mystery of the womb, the mystery is wrapped in a simple tone composed by Wolfgang Plagge, a creative Norwegian composer who has enriched our liturgy. His style is modern, yet clearly built on tradition, often with elements of folk music.

We repeat a Christmas antiphon for the Canticle of Vigils: *Before the red dawn was created, before the time came to be, he was: he willed to be born today as our Lord and Savior.*

The world has celebrated New Year with fireworks at midnight. Some of us wake up from the noise of our neighbors and go to different parts of the monastery to see the flashing beauty against the cold sky. Situated on a flat island in the middle of a broad fjord, we enjoy the splendor far away and close by. It is a joyful thrill, for me a mystery from childhood, when my parents woke me up and carried me to the window so I could see.

After five minutes I go back to bed, awaiting with greater expectation the singing of Vigils, a different entering into reality and meaning.

What I am most grateful for, is . . .

The New Year chapter after Lauds shares our gratefulness from the year past and hopes for the year ahead. I am full of gratitude, yet my sisters have even more and other things to share. Listening to them expands my gratefulness.

The Mother of God. In my heart this is a day of special prayer. At Wrentham, the monastery I entered in the US, it was a day of recollection with adoration of the Blessed Sacrament all day. At Tautra we keep one hour of exposition and adoration every morning and do not have special days of recollection. This hour is a cornerstone in our busy community life, giving priority to the simple, quiet being in the presence of Christ. Nothing else. On this solemnity my monastic childhood follows me with a special feeling, and I try to take extra time for prayer during the day. It is good to start the New Year in open trust.

These darkest weeks of the year the light is most beautiful. The sun rises about 10 a.m. but needs half an hour to climb above the distant hills and spread its rays. The sun stays low, only three degrees up in the sky, as if she is so sleepy that she cannot decide whether to stay in bed or rise, just lying on the hills, slowly moving southwards and going back to bed before we pray None at 2:30 p.m. The light is completely horizontal, very, very soft. Two hours of dawn and two hours of dusk spread splendid colors over the sky: peach and orange, pink and turquoise, red and yellow, blue, white, and grey. How did God ever get the idea of creating such beauty for us?

The whole landscape is painted. White and black hills across the fjord become pink. Ten or twenty windows in the town across the fjord shine like stars as the sun rises. The fields glow gently yellow. The fjord changes constantly into different shades of blue, green, white, grey, pink, and yellow on the northern side, reflecting the sun in a broad golden band on the southern side. When I take a walk in the afternoon, the sun has already set. I walk towards the south and west, the most solitary part of the island, walking towards the sunset half the way, with a glowing sky over the hills behind the distant city of Trondheim. The distance makes the line of hills and mountains sharp and beautiful. As I return towards east the orange glow from the southwest reflects in the rocks of the shore.

This last day of the Christmas Octave is the last with the festive table where we sit facing one another. Tomorrow we are back to sitting in one line looking out on the fjord. This view is so precious that we all want the full view of the fjord during our meals. Sitting around the table is a gift of communion, especially for the talking meal at Christmas. It is a nice change. When sitting with the back towards the fjord, you still see the landscape reflected in the windows. And more: our monastery is full of small interior gardens. Behind the reflecting window is a garden, and behind is another window through which you see the scriptorium and the garden behind the scriptorium and the window behind that garden. A mystery enveloped in a mystery in a mystery. The gift of this beauty is a main feature of our monastic day; we never tire of receiving it and marveling at it: Look! Have you seen?

Human life is human life inside and outside the monastery. Monastic life is meant to hinder you from running away from yourself. The silence and solitude give plenty of opportunity to meet me and myself. It can be tough. There is much pain needed to make us fully human and Christ-like. The beauty of Tautra helps us to bear that pain. If you feel down, you can look up, look out, go out, and receive the vast sky above and around you, finding again your trust in the Loving God who created all this. Even on a grey, stormy day, you can find blue spots between the clouds, holes of hope. Enjoying the humor of the fjord playing ocean in the gale, gushing towards the shore with thundering voice.

Each of our seven interior gardens has a special character, giving a variety in a small space. Architecture, landscape, and nature influence us more than we may be aware of. We experienced this so keenly when we moved from the old farmhouses into our new monastic building. Suddenly our framework was what we recognized as monastic, and it gave a good support for living this life. Seven years in three small houses had special gifts for us and were important for forming us as a community. Having to cross the yard between the houses so many times a day opened my mind to the reality of weather, wind, and waves. I have made it my habit still to walk through the gardens every day, year round. It broadens the experience of walls and form and space. I start using the diagonal path through the rose garden on my way to Vigils. Nothing wakes you up like half a minute of fresh air. This is my reality check. Moving for a moment out of the security of a nice warm home, risking the reality beyond my control, with strong winds, rain or snow—or shining stars and Northern Lights in a breathtaking dance.

Christmastide lasts another week or two. We celebrate Epiphany on January 6 with a party, either with our monks coming from Munkeby, the Cistercian monastery in our neighboring town, or with our friends from the Support Group for our monastery, those who help us selling soaps and creams during the market of Saint Olav in July.

I like the wisdom of the Church expressed in keeping the Epiphany and the Baptism of Christ to round off the Christmas season. We live the mystery of the incarnation three times a day in the prayer of the Angelus. This rhythm of remembrance helps me realize more deeply the gift of God's love in Jesus' becoming a human being like us. It is like stepping outside for a moment and discovering the blue spot between the clouds. Adoring the newborn baby, Jesus, our God. Trying to take in the global aspect of the story of the wise men.

There is so much searching in this story. So much openness to the unknown. The season helps me: The light, the wind, the clouds, the rain, the low, glowing sun, and the black or blue sky, a surprising and uncontrollable reality, connecting the protection of the tiny baby and the God beyond the cosmos. The longer the night, the more precious is the light, and the more you become aware of both light and darkness. Just like the alternations in the life of prayer.

January is the time of heavy storms and gales. The hurricanes seldom reach us without being softened by the mountains around the fjord.

You stormy winds putting his word into action, we sing in the psalms. Why should I judge the strong winds to be bad? Yet I do pray they will not do too much harm.

Sometime after Epiphany we take down the Christmas trees and decorations. It is hard to let go of all the extra lights in this dark season. *Back to oatmeal and the coarse shirt,* we say in Norway when Christmas is finally over. The ordinary food and simplicity of monastic life is a new gift of the new year. Simplicity clears the way for the deeper realities of life.

We are back to ordinary time also in the liturgy, and we try to make January a more ordinary month on many levels. For that to happen, we take some extra measures, closing the guesthouse, having no volunteers, and taking extra time for reading and prayer. Few visitors find their way to the island these short winter days. Then suddenly, on a very ordinary Thursday, an hour before the winter sun will rise, the door opens as we are singing our communion song. A group enters the church, bringing a draft with a mixture of fresh, cold air and cigarette smoke. They quietly sit down. We have our silent thanksgiving after the communion, the prayer, the blessing, the dismissal, and continue our thanksgiving. Our guests remain through the office of Tierce. As we leave the church I catch a glimpse of the men and women. Sure enough, it is Roger and his guests.

Saint Joseph sent Roger to us in 1999. We had arrived on Tautra a few days earlier and were trying to find a carpenter who could make a bell tower for us. It was only three weeks before the foundation Mass and blessing of our bell. Three local carpenters had no time to do the job, and we were discussing whom we could ask. We also needed an apartment for our chaplain, who would arrive shortly. We decided to start a novena to Saint Joseph. Being a carpenter, he should know how to help us with our needs.

Before we ended our chapter meeting, there was a knock on the door. Two young men in blue overalls were standing on the porch: "We are carpenters. We thought maybe you would need help?" That was Roger and his cousin Frode. Three weeks later the bell arrived and found its home in a new bell tower. A real bell and a bell tower immediately made it clear that this was a monastery. Later that day we had also found a flat for our chaplain on a neighboring farm.

Roger quickly found out when we had our prayer before lunch, and whenever he had any business excuse to come, he would come right before prayer and join us in the living room we had made our chapel. "Do you allow children?" he asked, and brought his one-year-old son, then his whole family, then his extended family, then his friends.

"When *you* say a blessing, you mean it," he said. "You accept people as they are, so with you it is OK to be different."

Roger was the grandson of one of our old neighbors. His wife's farm is on the Frosta peninsula, close to our island. Roger and Janne Mette renovated the hay barn of their farm and made it a catering restaurant and a conference center. He bought a van and started bringing groups of his guests to the monastery, always to attend an Office. It is a joy when Roger and his groups turn up in our church.

One morning it is snowing. Snowflakes are falling softly and quietly in a stream of light over the bell tower and the cross. Snow means extra work, but that is OK. These crystals make the world new. Shoveling the handicap ramp up to the church before Lauds is a joyful duty, making it safe for the Lord to arrive in an unknown and unexpected visitor. The snow covers the landscape; everything becomes clean and shiny, another Paradise. Most often the winds bringing the snow are so strong that the snow hardly falls down until it reaches the woodlands of Frosta a few miles to the East. On good years we get enough snow to go skiing for a few days.

"Er det skisko?" (Are those ski shoes?), asked Sr. Anne, who had a break in her Norwegian course.

Yes: I explained the different words for shoes and boots and snowshoes. Did she know how to ski? She had done downhill skiing, but never cross country, which was her dream.

She wore my shoe size, and we took a three-minute skiing class in the guest refectory. I showed her the skis and the sticks. Now there were two of us to ski this course. Nobody else will try skiing on this flat, small island, so we must make the tracks ourselves, again and again, since the wind covers the tracks before we return home.

Norwegians are born with skis on their feet. It is close to the truth. We bring babies out in sheepskin and sled connected to the skiing parent as soon as they are a few months old. When you can walk, you can ski. For the rest of your life, coming back to these sliding movements is a joy to the body and the soul. It is a freedom and an experience of unity with nature that is very special. You feel every change in the ground, and you must be prepared for surprises under the snow: your body becomes like a spring that moves as needed.

Skiing at Tautra means skiing along the shore, a new experience for me when we came here. Listening to the water and bathing in the low sun reflected in the fjord is so different from skiing in the mountains and the woods. A quick afternoon skiing is a blessing for the mind and body for the whole year. There is nothing like these diagonal movements combined with the cool, fresh air and white, soft snow.

Every Friday morning we sing Psalm 50 (51) at Lauds, with the verse, *Oh, purify me, then I shall be clean; O wash me, I shall be whiter than snow.* The image of the psalm becomes more graphic and clean when you really dive into the snow landscape and let yourself become one with it.

Sometimes we give presentations to the sisters from what we focus on in reading during January. One year I titled my presentation, *What is so special with the special places?* The practice of silence in our house is a matter we focus on at certain intervals. Our prioress had recently reminded us about keeping better silence, and as I reflected on this, I realized how much we were slipping away from silence in the rooms that our Constitutions call *the special places*, where we should be extra vigilant about keeping silence. Why? I wondered, why do we consider some rooms, some places, some surroundings more holy than others, so much that we change our behavior when we enter these rooms?

The *special places* mentioned in our Constitutions are the church, the cloister, the refectory, and the scriptorium. Even the silence in the church is not so evident in our time, but our guests and visitors respect the small sign we have, saying "This is the House of God, the Gate of Heaven: Please respect the silence in this sacred place." We ourselves enter the church using Holy Water to make the Sign of the Cross and bowing deep before the altar as we enter. These simple movements help us to enter a mindset that should be ours all day, focusing on God more than on the practical tasks of the day. It is also easy when we enter any of the other special places in procession from the church, still in that same mindset. It is more difficult at other times of the day. Why is it important?

I think of it in terms of a constant learning of humility: respecting the silence in certain rooms connected to listening to the Word is a good discipline. My thoughts and words are not as important as I may think. I can wait, hold back, learn to listen more to God, more to others.

As I was praying about this, trying to listen deeper, a local saying came up in me: Go hiking, and you will never be in a bad mood. *(Ut på tur, aldri sur!)* Yes, there is a connection: When we go hiking, a favorite weekend activity in Norway, we often stop for a moment, saying: *Listen to the silence!*

This awe in the face of nature reminds me of the greatness of God, and the same awe and silence should fill me as I move through the monastery during the day, resting in the smallness of my being.

Beginning a New Year means looking back and looking forward. It is time to see that everything needed for the book-keeper is in the books, and checking where we are with costs and prices. It is too soon to see how we did economically last year, but there is work to catch up on after finishing the inventory of the soap department. It is also time for the first big orders we need for our production in the coming months. The presence of new sisters entering this work means more computer knowledge and more effective planning. I enjoy seeing how we can simplify the work.

Looking forward means making soap for the *Olsok* historical market at the end of July, for the Feast of Saint Olav (995–1030), the patron of Norway. He is caring well for us. Since our first year at Tautra our biggest sales have been at this historical market at the medieval Archbishop's Palace, next to Nidaros Cathedral in Trondheim. Our friends in the Support Group, the people who prayed our monastery into being, help us sell our products at the fair. We make all the cold-process soap and the balm needed for the market during the first weeks of the year.

Making soap is about transformation, like the life in Christ. What is more fitting for nuns? Transformation is the key in soap making. You start with lye and oil, you mix, and a chemical process starts. When this process is finished, there is no more lye or oil, only soap.

We choose good ingredients for our soaps. Good hygiene is basic in the production of skin products. The skin is the surface of the whole body, protection and sensitivity, and closely connected to the psyche, important for all human life. Soap is cleansing and disinfecting, like the sacrament of reconciliation. Cleaning the skin is necessary so the skin can do its job.

"Wash your hands! Wash your hands! Wash your hands!" This is the best advice the doctors give in January, a month full of colds and flu. It is a nice job for us to provide soap with prayer and love.

We emphasize accuracy when weighing up the ingredients. For a 52-kilo batch of soap it is hard work. Just like vigilance in the Christian life, it is about body and soul, heart and thought, structure, faithfulness, and good habits. To get good soap you must love doing it. Enthusiasm helps, combined with steadfastness and peace.

It takes five days to make our cold-process soap, and it needs three weeks of drying before we can box and label and sell it. We weigh up the oils and mix the lye on Monday morning. Mixing the lye takes extra vigilance, since this is a dangerous work, like life itself. Tuesday morning is the time for mixing. We melt the oils Monday evening, and they cool down to body temperature during the night. The mixed lye has cooled down faster and needs heating up to get to the same temperature. There are some hectic minutes when the temperatures are right and the mixing starts in the huge kettle filled with oils. As soon as we see a tracing in the thickening soup, we add the essential oils, aroma, and herbs. Now the saponification thickens the soup fast, and we pour it into the soap mold. We cover it with waxed paper, towels, and blankets and put it to sleep in a closet. We have done our best; now we must wait, letting the chemical process work alone in the dark. Friday or Saturday it is time to cut. It is always different, and a thrill to see if we got a beautiful and good soap.

The patience in the making of a person into the likeness of Christ is far more demanding, but making soap is a help to understand that you can only do so much on your own, and it takes a team to do it well.

January 20 is the memorial of a modern saint from our own Order, Cyprian Michael Tansi. A Nigerian priest, he felt called to monastic life and entered Mount St. Bernard Abbey in England. His fellow monks described him as an ordinary monk. I love this ordinariness, the fact that holiness is lived in a hidden way. It helps me to step back, to open up for the unseen and unnoticed holiness in people around me.

As January moves into its last week, we have feasts piling up: January 25 is the conversion of Saint Paul. The next day is the solemnity of the founders of our Cistercian Order, Saints Robert, Alberic, and Stephen. Our blessed local Archbishop Eystein (+1188) has to wait until the next day, though his feast is also the 26th.

The conversion of Saint Paul challenges our daily conversion. The melodies for the antiphons for Lauds bring the texts deep into the heart: *As he approached Damascus, suddenly a light from the sky flashed around him, and he fell to the ground.*

Few of us may have an experience as dramatic as the one of Saint Paul. In a society increasingly turned away from God, we often hear dramatic stories of how Jesus breaks into a person's life. Going for a walk on Tautra on a grey and ordinary day, I may have the experience of a sudden light flashing around me—although it is "only" the sun flooding through a hole in the black cloud. My friend calls it "Holy-Spirit-light." It seems fitting to see everything that happens around us as God's message. Always look up, and there is a blue spot lifting your spirits to gratitude and openness.

Now get up, Saul, and go into the city. There somebody will tell you what you shall do.

The antiphons work like *lectio divina*, the slow, meditative reading of Scripture. As you sing them year after year, although only once or twice a year, they sing themselves into your heart and pop up at fitting times to give you a message: Get up! Go! Wait! You are not in charge, you will be led by God. Christ will tell somebody to lead you in your blindness, and you will regain your sight.

Living in a community or a family is a special grace. For better and for worse, Christ is forming us through the other and the others. We need the question posed to Saul: *Saul, Saul, why are you persecuting me?* Will it ever teach us to stop our critical thoughts about others?

Starting a new foundation in a country where there was no monastery of the Benedictine family, we have put much effort into making a good liturgy, using what already exists in Norwegian, but also composing new music when needed. Some of us have experienced that we—to our surprise—can do it, can receive the inspiration, can express our tradition while using influence from different traditions. I often think of how the Norwegian Lutheran hymn tradition and folk music have formed my prayer and my musical language. I am deeply grateful for my mother, who sang hymns during her work in the house. Her example taught me to love them and learn them by heart. The hymns became my continual prayer.

The Norwegian folk tunes have much in common with Gregorian Chant, and with English, Irish, and American folk music. A big inspiration for me is the liturgical music of Sr. Edith Scholl of Wrentham, happy, contemplative, and modern.

Approaching January 26, the solemnity of the founders of our Order of Cîteaux, Saints Robert, Alberic, and Stephen, a joy creeps into my whole body. Celebrating our origin deepens and strengthens our identity and our unity with sisters and brothers of the Cistercian Order through the centuries. I like to read some of the early documents from the twelfth century on this feast, especially the *Exordium Parvum*, which the first generation of Cistercians wrote and addressed to us, so that we should know how everything was properly done from the beginning. It is like Saint Luke and Saint John, so clearly expressing that they are writing to *us* so that we may believe. This direct relationship and communication with those who went before us I find very inspiring.

Nine hundred years ago this group of monks was called to leave their fairly comfortable life in the Abbey of Molesme to start from scratch at Cîteaux, finding their way in greater poverty, greater economic and social independence, greater simplicity, greater authenticity. How do we do it today?

This year I read about Stephen Harding, one of the three saints we celebrate on this date and the third abbot of Cîteaux. I think he might have been the most important of the three. Suddenly I notice that his father or grandfather might have been in the service of King Harold of England. Oh? This was the king who fought our Norwegian king Harald Hardråde, whose son Olav Kyrre built the Romanesque cathedral over the grave of Saint Olav in Trondheim, the columns of which we can still see. A hundred years after the battle of Hastings, in 1166, the first Cistercians came from Fountains to Norway, and not long after that some of them probably went to Munkeby. Fascinating connections.

In honor of this solemnity we have a coffee break after Mass. Sr. Renata asks, "Can you tell some memories from OUR foundation, from the early days?"

Leaving the established life in our monasteries, moving into the unknown, is certainly a tasking adventure. Probably we still do not know what this is, what God is calling us to become. We may see some sketchy features of Tautra Mariakloster, we experience the growth of the community and enjoy the monastic church and buildings, we realize the importance of the warm welcome we have had and still enjoy. What is the enculturation of Cistercian life in the Norwegian culture? It will take many years before we can see and express what it is and to what degree we have been able to answer this part of our calling.

Memories of our foundation? I see the small group of our friends in the Support Group who were still at the airport with the bishop as Sr. Marjoe and I landed after a four-hour delay— waiting with Norwegian flags. Arriving at Tautra, where our friends had the fire burning in the fireplace and the flag outside to welcome us. The first days before the furniture came, when we carried our chairs from one house to the other for every prayer and every meal. Of course also the first guests, the fifteen students who woke us up at 9:30 p.m. the day after our arrival, asking if they might sleep in our boathouse. They were rowing the fjord this February night, giving up the goal of a Saturday-night dance in Trondheim because of the rain and heavy headwinds. We let them sleep in the empty house where the chapel was, and when we came in for Vigils the whole house smelled of tar from the boat. We gave them oatmeal and caramels from Our Lady of the Mississippi Abbey for breakfast; that was all we had. The next year another group came back with the same teacher. That time they arrived safely for Vespers, in good weather.

Sancta Maria de Tuta Insula is the name of our monastery, meaning Saint Mary of the safe harbor. Nobody on the island had experienced people knocking at the door seeking safe harbor. Our Lady prepared us for a life of hospitality. More than fifteen years later their teacher turned up to celebrate Christmas with us, surprised to find the big beautiful monastery and the community doubled in size.

Sr. Renata had finished her second part of the language course. We try to use Norwegian at work, and I started out in Norwegian with what I wanted to say. After two minutes I stopped. Her smile said, "I do not understand, but it is OK." " Sorry," I said, "You didn't get it. I'll go slower." She laughed: "No, I didn't get it, but it is so lovely to listen to your language—I love it!"

We all struggle with the languages, English and Norwegian being the languages of the community, and French, Dutch, Polish, Vietnamese, and Flemish being the other mother tongues. I think it is part of our vocation to live the frustration and challenge so many immigrants and refugees experience in our time. Even when you think you have learned a language, you do not understand what people say, and they do not understand what you are saying. In my head I often say, "Your Norwegian is fine. I just don't understand which vowels you are saying and which consonants and what words—but your accent is very good!—And what do they think about my English and French?"

The international reality of our community well reflects these January feasts. Saint Paul, who went far to preach the

Gospel, Saint Stephen from England, who became abbot of Cîteaux in France. Our Archbishop Eskild of Lund (then Denmark, now Sweden), who was a friend of Saint Bernard and had been to Clairvaux. The gathering of Scandinavian bishops for his ordination in 1133 probably prompted several Cistercian foundations in Scandinavia. Our later archbishop, Saint Eystein of Trondheim, studied at St. Victor in France and spent a few years in the Cistercian abbey of Fountains in England. We are all linked together, and these feasts remind us of the history that shaped our reality today.

January 29 I open the email: *Today the sun is up 7 hours,* writes our friend Olav Arne, who helps us with the gardens. I check the farmers' log book: Yes, he is right, to the minute! Exactly seven hours. In four weeks the day has become 2½ hours longer. The winter darkness is over; the sun is climbing higher on the sky every day. We can already see the landscape turning pink on the other side of the fjord during Mass. The fjord is green, turning into light blue, then dark blue as the landscape turns white and black.

Out of Darkness

A new year, born out of darkness
like Christ in the stall

A new beginning, born from sleep
like Christ calming the storm

Life unknown in heavy winds
following him to the Cross

Being formed, morning by morning
like Christ, going out to pray.

February

Daylight Returns

Sr. Anne Elizabeth Sweet, OCSO

I will turn the darkness before them into light. (Isa 42:16)

It was February when I first came to Norway in 2005, and to be honest, I didn't want to come. I had made other plans for March of that year: spending some weeks being tutored by a scholar of our order, something I had long awaited. But when my abbess asked me if I would come to Norway to teach, I didn't think that I could say "no" to what I had been asked to do, especially since I would be teaching my sisters. The abbess had said that I would not be able to do the tutorial, since I was also going to Nigeria to teach for three months in the summer. It was hard to give that up.

I will never forget how I felt sitting in the plane at O'Hare, waiting for takeoff. Why did I ever say that I would do this? I really didn't want to go to Norway in February. I had heard about the long dark days of winter in Norway—although, as I discovered, February days at Tautra were the same as at home. It is amazing how quickly the light already returns in January. My friends at home were asking me what I had done to be sent to Norway (nothing), as if to imply that this was the equivalent of being sent to Siberia, where I would surely die from the harsh winters. I must admit that I shared some of that fear. To my surprise, Tautra turned out to be much warmer than Iowa, thanks to the Gulf Stream. And contrary to what my family and friends still believe after fifteen years, I do *not* live in an igloo! and there are *no* polar bears romping about in our back yard!

As we drove home from the airport in Trondheim, I remember being surprised that I could recognize the meaning of some words on various signs, as they were the same as in German. I remember experiencing firsthand what the foundresses had talked about for the previous six years while they were living in the old farmhouses: what it was like to go from one house (where the chapel was) to the other house (where the refectory was) three times a day in procession regardless of the weather, with all seven of us changing shoes in the tiny entrance way to whichever house we were entering. Since we slept in three different houses, the back-and-forth movement was even more frequent than that.

And the food. Since most of the sisters were American, the food was mostly American. However, I do remember one Norwegian fish dish—I was clueless as to what it was and at a loss as to how to eat it. Fortunately, I happened to be the reader during dinner that day, which meant that I ate after the meal; that was great, as I could ask someone what to do. "How do you eat this?" I asked one of the sisters. "I don't!" she replied! Sound ridiculous? I've thought of this incident many times in relation to the adjustments our Asian sister must now make to the food that the Westerners cook and enjoy.

When I came in 2005, one of the American foundresses had discerned that she was not called to remain at Tautra and had returned to our abbey in Iowa. One of the Norwegian sisters had likewise determined that she was not called to transfer her stability to Tautra and was preparing to return to her abbey in France when I arrived. Among her jobs was that of accompanist for the Offices. I won't say organist, because at that time, we had only an electric keyboard.

I don't know if sharing the community's experience of the loss of two foundresses was a factor, but to my great surprise I became aware of a growing and persistent sense of a call to become part of the community at Tautra. "Is this real?" I thought. "How do I know?" I wondered. Like many before me, I asked, "Lord, give me a sign if it is real." Walking in the ruins of the old medieval monastery one day and repeating my prayer for a sign, I stepped down into what had been one of the smaller rooms adjacent to the church. Turning, I saw a small bright yellow flower under the stone step—so bright against the snow—the only flower in sight. When I brought it home, Sister Hanne-Maria told me that while it was the first flower to grow in the spring, it was much too early for them to appear. I had my sign.

I told the sisters about my experiences and my desire to return, but also that I needed time to just be with such an unexpected turn of events. I also said that I didn't think that I could give any more thought to it while I was in Nigeria, as I thought that my commitment there would take all of my attention. To my surprise, the thought of Norway came up during my prayer literally every day that I was in Nigeria. Even more of a surprise was the discovery of a book on the Norwegian language in the library at Abakaliki!

It was only in May of 2006 that I was able to return, two days before the annual celebration of Norway's national day. But February will always be associated in my mind with my first experience of Norway: "by paths they have not known I will guide them. I will turn the darkness before them into light" (Isa 42:16).

February 2:
The Feast of the Presentation of the Lord

The Lord will come with mighty power and give light to the eyes of all who serve him (from the opening canticle of the Mass with the blessing of candles).

February 2 is preeminently a feast of light. Today, forty days after Jesus' birth, we recall the presentation of the infant Jesus in the Temple, when the prophet Simeon acclaimed him as "a light for revelation" (Luke 2:32). In former times, before the post-conciliar revision of the liturgical calendar in 1969, this day marked the end of the Christmas season, during which we celebrated the birth of the One who is the true Light of the world (John 1:4, 5, 9). Today's feast reminds us that Jesus remains with us as the true light regardless of whatever darkness God's people—and indeed the world—experience.

Today's emphasis on light is likewise manifest in the long-time tradition of blessing candles on this day and distributing them to people for their homes. I remember how at home blessed candles were kept by a crucifix that was used when the priest came to anoint the sick or to bring them Communion. We also lit blessed candles during times when we prayed for God's special protection, such as during severe weather or threatening hurricanes (I grew up on the Gulf Coast). I have been in parishes and communities where people brought candles from home that adorned a special place of prayer to be blessed on February 2.

Here at Tautra, we gather in the cloister for the blessing of candles and go in procession with lighted candles to the church for the celebration of the Eucharist. Our candles, placed at the foot of the altar, burn throughout the day. Our celebration of the Feast actually begins at Vigils, our first prayer of the day, at 4:20 a.m. "Your light has come, Jerusalem! The Lord's glory shines over you. In your light shall all peoples walk," one of the antiphons proclaims. And in these words, we hear the call to live and be what we profess to be, and to reflect the Light of the Lord to all who come to us.

Some of the most beautiful sermons of our Cistercian Fathers were written for this feast; these are often used as the second nocturn reading at Vigils. Those of the twelfth-century abbot Guerric of Igny are among my favorites. In his first sermon for this feast, Guerric writes,

> Could anyone hold up a lighted candle in his hands on this day without at once remembering that old man [Simeon] who on this same day took up in his arms Jesus, God's Word, clothed in flesh like a candle-flame clothed in wax, and affirmed him to be the Light which would be

a beacon for the Gentiles? Surely he was that burning and radiant lamp which bore witness to the Light. For this purpose he came in the Spirit, who had filled him, into the temple: that he might receive, O God, your Loving-Kindness in the midst of your temple and declare him to be Loving-Kindness indeed and the Light of your own people. Truly, O holy Simeon, in the quiet contentment of old age you carried this Light not simply in your hands but in the very dispositions of your heart.[1]

Guerric goes on to exhort his monks,

> Come then, my brethren, give an eye to that candle burning in Simeon's hands. Light your candles too by borrowing from that Light; for these candles I speak of are the lamps which the Lord orders us to have in our hands. Come to him and be enlightened, so as to be not merely carrying lamps but to be the very lamps yourselves, shining inside and out, for yourselves and for your neighbors. Be a lamp then in heart, in hand, in lips. The lamp in your heart will shine for you; the lamp in your hand or on your lips will shine out for your neighbors. The lamp in the heart is loving faith; the lamp in the hand is the example of good works; the lamp on the lips is edifying speech.[2]

The editor of Guerric's sermons adds a touching detail to the celebration of this feast in a footnote: "The monks received newly-blessed candles which they lighted from the light that had been kept alive in the sanctuary lamp since the lighting and blessing of the new fire on the previous paschal night."[3] Thus the Light that they carried was the Paschal Light, the Light of the Risen Jesus. It is this light that we, too, must carry and become.

---

[1] Guerric of Igny, Sermon 1.2, in *Liturgical Sermons*, vol. 1, translated by Monks of Mount Saint Bernard Abbey, CF 8 (Kalamazoo, MI: Cistercian Publications, 1971), 101.

[2] Guerric, Sermon 1.3 (CF 8:102–3).

[3] Guerric, CF 8:99, n. 1.

A further note on the celebration of this feast at Tautra: in 1997, Saint Pope John Paul II designated February 2 as a day of prayer for consecrated religious, a day on which they could "renew their commitment and rekindle the fervor which should inspire their offering of themselves to the Lord."[4]

So on this day, we go to Trondheim to join with all the other religious in our diocese for a day together in accord with the directives of John Paul II: "They are invited to celebrate together solemnly the marvels which the Lord has accomplished in them, to discover by a more illumined faith the rays of divine beauty spread by the Spirit in their way of life, and to acquire a more vivid consciousness of their irreplaceable mission in the Church and in the world."[5]

"All the other religious" is, in fact, not so many. In 2018, there were the fourteen of us from Tautra, our five brothers from Munkeby (since 2009 a community of our brothers from Cîteaux), the Brigittine sisters from Trondheim, and the four women belonging to St. Bonifatius's Institute in Levanger. The three Sisters of the Most Blessed Trinity serving in Molde were unable to join us that year. The day began with lunch and included a presentation by Pater Egil Mogstad, pastor of St. Olav's Domkirke (cathedral) in Trondheim, who is also a Third Order Dominican; time for discussion followed. In addition, there was time for private prayer in the beautiful new cathedral.

All of us joined with the local parishioners for the celebration of the Eucharist with the blessing and procession with candles. That was particularly fitting, since John Paul II had wished that the day serve also "to promote a knowledge of and esteem for the consecrated life by the entire People of God." Their witness of our renewal of commitment was to be a sign that "the life of special consecration, in its many forms, is thus at the service of the baptismal consecration of all the faithful. In contemplating the gift of the consecrated life, the

[4] Message of the Holy Father John Paul II for the First World Day of Prayer for Consecrated Life, January 6, 1997, 1.

[5] John Paul II, Message, 4.

Church contemplates her own intimate vocation of belonging only to her Lord. . . ."[6]

Our Cistercian Constitutions speak of the hidden apostolic fruitfulness of our cloistered life: "By fidelity to their monastic way of life, which has its own hidden mode of apostolic fruitfulness, nuns perform a service for God's people and the whole human race" (Const 3.4). This statement is something I often reflect on, and indeed I can say I experience it, primarily in our intercessory prayer for all God's people—not only when we pray the Divine Office together, but also in our silent prayer throughout the day. Sometimes, especially when I am doing manual work, a particular person or group of people will come to mind, for example, those in prison. I see this as the inspiration of the Spirit to pray for people in prison, and so I do, especially for a prisoner most in need at that particular time. And I believe in the power of my prayer for that person, no matter where he or she is.

Another way our hidden apostolic fruitfulness manifests itself, I believe, is simply by our faithful witness to a life of prayer in the praise of God. Who sees this? Well, here at Tautra, the countless groups of tourists and visitors to the island who come to see the church and join us for a time of prayer. Norway is a very secular country. Most Norwegians are nominal Lutherans, and many others say they are not sure if there is a God or, simply, that they don't believe. I believe that many are touched by their experience of being here; it is evident on their faces. And they tell us that they experience such a deep peace when they are here. Perhaps the beginnings of faith are being awakened in them. Such is our prayer, such is our service for the people here.

The February 2 Day for Consecrated Religious always concludes with a festive dinner. It is a great opportunity to connect with other religious in our diocese, to renew friendships and support in our various ministries. Our celebration in 2018 also had a note of sadness, as the four members of Bonifatius

---

[6] John Paul II, Message, 3.

Institute serving in Levanger would be leaving Norway in June. A decline in membership in the Institute had led to the closing of the house. Some of these sisters had been in Norway for thirty years and had in fact been at the airport to welcome our sisters when they arrived in 1999 to establish the foundation of Tautra Mariakloster. And now we say farewell to them.

Their departure will mean the loss of consecrated religious in the city of Levanger, about an hour's drive from Tautra. The declining numbers of many religious institutes calls us to fervent prayer for an increase in vocations, as we do each day at Vespers: for our own community, for our brothers at Munkeby (near Levanger), and for the church at large. Our hope is that you, the reader, will likewise join us in this prayer.

Parish Visits

In your light we see light. (Ps 36:9)

Another opportunity for us "to promote a knowledge of . . . the consecrated life" among Catholic Norwegians arose in conjunction with our fundraising to build an addition to our monastery now that we are fourteen in a house built for sixteen! This new addition will have eight cells or bedrooms, four of them for sick or elderly members, equipped so that we can care for them at home until death.

It was suggested to us by an adviser from outside the community who had been involved with the Iowa fundraising campaign to build Tautra Mariakloster twenty years ago that we make an appeal in the local parishes, as we did in Dubuque. However, there are several significant differences between then and now. One is the fact that Dubuque, Iowa, is a very Catholic area. Catholics are a minority in Norway, less than four percent of the total population. The Catholic Church in Norway is an international one, and in fact there are more Polish Catholics in Norway than Norwegian ones! In most parishes, Sunday Masses are celebrated in Norwegian, Polish, and English. Some parishes also have Masses in Vietnamese and Tagalog, among other languages.

The diocese of Trondheim to which we belong comprises 56,458 square kilometers and consists of five parishes. By contrast, the Dubuque archdiocese has 166 parishes at the time of this writing, in a geographical area comprising some 45,000 square kilometers. Twenty years ago there were no doubt more parishes. We did not visit all of them, but we could easily drive when we did.

There are two Catholic parishes within an hour and a half drive away from Tautra. St. Torfinn's in Levanger, one hour away, is technically our home parish. It is also the home parish of the two Catholics living in our nearby town of Frosta. St. Olav's in Trondheim, an hour and a half drive, is our diocesan cathedral. The remaining three parishes in the diocese are several hours away.

Thus it is easy to understand why we are referred to as among the Catholics living in the diaspora or minority situation. It is the reality of the Church in Norway, where many priests must minister not only in the parish where they live but in one or more mission sites as well. Happily for us, there is an organization within the Catholic Church in Germany called Bonifatiuswerk. Its purpose is to financially assist Catholics in the diaspora. In addition, it develops educational material and material for catechesis in order to support parishes in their mission to strengthen and to pass on our faith. It was largely because of their help and the generosity of German Catholics that we were able to build our monastery. They have continued to help us through the years. For this we are most grateful.

As part of our fundraising efforts for enlarging the monastery we visited parishes in Oslo and Bergen as well, speaking at the Sunday Masses. Since we have sisters who speak Norwegian, Polish, Vietnamese, and English, we were generally able to manage. We wanted our efforts not just to be about fundraising, but also to be an occasion to tell people about our life and our vocation, to let them know that we are there on Tautra, that we are praying for them, and that they are most welcome in our guesthouse for a time of retreat.

To our surprise, we discovered that many, especially among the people outside of the Trondheim-Levanger area, did not know that we were here—including the priests, among whom there is a high turnover; many of them come from other countries. I was happy to observe in subsequent months more Catholics coming for retreats, many for the first time.

The parishes we visited welcomed us warmly, and at the Masses the priests introduced us by quoting John Paul II, who wrote, "The consecrated life is at the very heart of the Church, as a decisive element for her mission, since it manifests 'the inner nature of the Christian calling' and the striving of the whole Church as Bride towards union with her one spouse."

Yes, we are here, striving to bear witness to that "inner nature of the Christian calling," both as individual nuns seeking union with Christ and as the local monastic church, as our Constitutions describe each community.

February 14:
Feast of Saints Cyril and Methodius
(826–869; 815–885)

I have given you as a covenant to the people, a light to the nations. (Isa 42:6)

Feast? I wondered that first February in 2005. It was a happy wondering, as it happened to be Lent, and we especially look forward to feasts at that time. My knowledge of Cyril and Methodius was rather scant, though I had known monks who bore their names. I knew only that they were missionaries from Eastern Europe and had something to do with an alphabet. And suddenly I was encountering them as patrons of Europe.

After I moved to Norway, I learned of more patron saints of Europe: Benedict of Nursia, Bridget of Sweden, Catherine of Siena, and Edith Stein (or Sister Teresa Benedicta of the Cross). Since Cistercians live by the Rule of Saint Benedict and I had been a Benedictine before becoming a Cistercian, Benedict and I had a long acquaintance. But some of the others were more or less new to me. And now, since I lived in Scandinavia, Europe's close neighbor, they were my patrons as well.

I belonged now to a part of the world that was new to me, even though I had traveled in France, Germany, and the United Kingdom. Both of my grandmothers were immigrants. My German maternal great-grandparents could not speak English. My paternal grandmother was British, straight from London. Now I was the immigrant, living in a new land, knowing only my sisters at Tautra who also came from the States.

The figure of Ruth easily comes to mind: "Your people shall be my people," Ruth the Moabitess said to Naomi, her widowed and childless Hebrew mother-in-law, as they returned to Bethlehem (Ruth 1:16). Ruth, also a widow, refused to heed Naomi's admonition that she stay in her own land with her own people and find a husband there. "Your people shall be my people," said Ruth as she willingly, out of love, accompanied Naomi. Ruth became the immigrant, living among a new people in a new land out of love and commitment to Naomi.

And so it was for each of the American foundresses of Tautra Mariakloster as well as for the sisters who entered later, whether from Europe or from Asia. For all of us, being in Norway means a new people, a new land, a new language, and to some extent a new culture. Each of us is called to make it our own, and that means relinquishing, letting go, at least to some extent, of what has previously been ours.

It has been twenty years since the foundresses arrived in Norway in February 1999. Sheryl and I came later, 2002 and 2006. My own experience is that we are still very American— perhaps because most of the foundresses are American.

Language is a particular problem. Although both our Liturgy of the Hours and our Mass are celebrated in Norwegian, and most of us understand what we are saying or hearing,

English is still our main language. We've all had Norwegian language courses of various kinds, but it is hard to learn a language that one doesn't use. We speak English to one another—or French, in the case of the French-speaking sisters. For me personally, it is difficult for me to speak Norwegian with sisters whom I've known for twenty-four years in English. Most Norwegians know and understand English, and many speak it fluently. I would even go so far to say that English is a second language in Norway. This doesn't help our learning to speak Norwegian!

Our new members come to us not knowing Norwegian, and some not knowing English, at least not very well. Our formation program is in English, so that means that many of them must also learn English as well. I teach several classes, and during a Scripture class one day, I suddenly realized that each of my four students was using a Bible in a language different from my own—and from one another's. It is a real challenge when trying to help them find texts!

In my own case, facility with conversational Norwegian is a real need. You can't learn a language you don't use. The biblical Norwegian that we know is not what people use in everyday life. I can speak Norwegian, but I lack the ease and spontaneity I would like to have. So I am looking for ways to remedy this.

Our new (non-American) prioress has said that addressing the language issue will be one of her first priorities: "Norway has welcomed our community for almost twenty years. It is a duty of gratitude to practice the language of the country not only outside but also among ourselves." So, now, as a community, we have a Norwegian class once a week.

It goes without saying that having a common language will unify our community and enable us to share at a deeper level. Saint Alberic, one of our Cistercian founders, is described in the *Exordium Parvum* as "a lover of the Rule and of the brethren" (IX.2). His confrere Saint Stephen is described as "a lover of the Rule and of the place" (XVII.3). And so each of us is called to be first and foremost within the community, as expressed by our vow of stability, where we bind ourselves to the local monastery until death. I always get reactions of surprise when I tell people not familiar with the Benedictine-Cistercian tradition that we will remain here in the monastery until death!

Being a lover of the people and the place is also applicable to our relationship with the people of the land. And certainly the same could be said of Cyril and Methodius in their missionary endeavors. How fitting, given Cyril and Methodius's role in spreading Christianity in Europe, that we look to them now as patrons of Europe. How fitting, living in a society and culture now described as post-Christian, that we implore their intercession for our country's return to Christian roots.

For some Norwegians, it is not so much a return, but rather an encounter with Christianity for the first time, as is the case of those who have had no religious upbringing whatsoever. Others had religious upbringing but found it a negative, stifling experience that lacked any joy. They therefore want no part of it. Others in this post-Christian society doubt the existence of God.

I was genuinely shocked on coming to Norway to learn of the "humanetisk konfirmasjon" for those with no religious affiliation. There is a period of preparation similar to Christian confirmation that focuses on a vision of life, ethics, humanism, human rights, and critical thinking. A ceremony takes place to mark the conclusion of the course, as well as family celebrations with a festive meal and many gifts. All of that is very good, but something is missing.

What about the sacrament as the completion of initiation into the Church? Even though in the Lutheran Church confirmation is not a sacrament, there is still the ecclesial dimension. What about the Holy Spirit as the power of God's work within us, which can really make a difference in our lives?

Yes, we need the intercession of Cyril and Methodius and all of our other patron saints. We need their Christian witness.

We need to recall their work in the spread of Christianity—and somehow, in the manner in which we are able as cloistered nuns, to be missionaries and witnesses to the Gospel of Christ.

Ash Wednesday: The Beginning of Lent

Your light shall break forth like the dawn. (Isa 58:8: 1st Reading of the Mass for Friday after Ash Wednesday)

Lent is a special time in the monastery as it is for all Christians. Saint Benedict, in fact, devotes a whole chapter to the topic, with emphasis on how the season is to be observed in the monastery. His opening words express his conviction that "the life of the monk ought to have about it all times the character of a Lenten observance" (RB 49.1).[7] These words may elicit dread and groans, perhaps in large part determined by our previous experiences of Lent. Self-denial, giving up, or doing without something we like to have and enjoy are not practices many of us readily embrace.

Benedict was well aware of this reality and accordingly continues in the second verse of this chapter, "since few have the virtue for that, we therefore urge that during the actual days of Lent the brethren keep their lives most pure and at the same time wash away during these holy days all the negligences of other times" (RB 49.2). He then goes on to list the practices that will help us to do just that. The holy season of Lent thus becomes a gift.

My own perspective on Lent was greatly enriched when several years ago I wrote a book of reflections on the responsorial psalms of the Mass for the Lenten season. I must admit that I approached the project with a bit of dread, expecting the Scriptures to be heavily oriented toward human sinfulness and

---

[7] Leonard J. Doyle, trans., *The Rule of Saint Benedict* (Collegeville, MN: Liturgical Press, 1948), 2001. RB verse references are cited from *RB 1980*, ed. and trans. Timothy Fry (Collegeville, MN: Liturgical Press, 1981).

failures. There is that, to be sure, but it is not the main focus. To my surprise, the overwhelming emphasis in the Lenten lectionary was on God's loving mercy, human sin notwithstanding.

In this light, I could better appreciate Benedict's recommended practices, all of which are directed toward enabling us to be focused on God and immersed in God's love. All of these practices can help us to counter or reverse the effects of the "negligences" of the choices we consciously, or perhaps more rightly said, unconsciously make in ordinary daily life.

Benedict's first practice is to "restrain ourselves from all vices" (RB 49.4). He assumes that we know what ours are, those patterns of thought and behavior that are not of God or of God's light, but rather increase the darkness of our hearts and bring darkness into the lives of the people around us. Some honest soul-searching and reflection is called for. What in our lives, our thoughts, our actions disturbs our inner peace and the peace and harmony that Benedict wants to prevail in the monastery? We are called to make choices, to choose NOT to act or think in what has become our habitual way if it is in a manner that is not of God. Choice is an act of our will, empowered by God's grace, for of ourselves we can do nothing but fall back into the habits that are not of God.

Benedict's second practice is to "give ourselves up to prayer with tears" (RB 49.4). Intense prayer, deeply felt, arising from both the awareness of our own powerlessness and the immense potential of God's power at work within us (Eph 3:20); tears of compunction, our hearts pierced by the realization of our sinfulness and failings, tears that beg for God's help, tears that overflow from the depths of a heart that has experienced the power of God's grace at work in one's life: "I can do all things through him who strengthens me" (Phil 4:13). Tears that overflow from the awareness of being deeply and personally loved by God.

Sacred Reading or *lectio* is the third Lenten practice recommended by Benedict. For the monastic this is usually Scripture.

We approach the Word of God with a listening heart, believing that it is a Word God speaks to us. The Scriptures are not only the story of God's people of old; they are our own story, a mirror for our own lives. Throughout the year our daily practice is to do Sacred Reading for at least thirty minutes a day. Benedict would have us do even more during Lent. In fact, in chapter 48 on the daily manual labor, he prescribes an additional hour each day for *lectio* during Lent (RB 48.10, 14). It was by doing *lectio* on the Lenten psalms that I came to recognize that the Lenten lectionary had more to say about God's mercy and love than about my sinfulness. In *lectio*, we are there to hear the word that God speaks and to recognize it as a word for us personally. *Lectio* is a personal encounter with the Lord.

This reality was powerfully and visually brought home to me during a recent visit to India, where in the churches I visited there was a niche with an open Bible in the wall behind the altar, parallel to a niche with the tabernacle on the other side. It was a beautiful way to emphasize that the Lord is present in his Word as well as in the Eucharist. In the adoration chapel where I often went to pray, several Bibles were available around the room, and I noticed how many people picked them up to read during prayer. The pages were well worn—and how I wish I could have read Malayalam to see what books were read the most! These people clearly recognized—and witnessed to—how important it is to spend time with the Word. And this was not a monastic setting!

Our Tautra community has a practice of doing *lectio* in common for thirty minutes each day during Lent. During this time, we read our Lenten book, which we receive on Ash Wednesday in accordance with Benedict's directive that each monastic receive a special book at the beginning of Lent, which is to be read from cover to cover (RB 48.15-16). In Benedict's day, this was probably a book of Scripture. In our own day, it can be any type of spiritual reading.

Benedict's fourth practice is "compunction of heart," that is, allowing our hearts to be pierced, broken open by the Word of God and the working of God's Spirit. It is not so much something that we do, but rather that the Lord's grace does within us, *if* we are receptive. "O that today you would listen to his voice! Do not harden your hearts," writes the psalmist (Ps 95:7-8). Benedict would have us begin Vigils each day with this verse, with this reminder to allow our hearts to be deeply touched and broken open by the Lord. In so doing, we yield ourselves to become moist and pliable clay in the hands of the divine potter. It is the beginning of the conversion and transformation that is ongoing until Christ is formed in us (Gal 4:19).

These first four practices enable us to be more focused on God and immersed in God's love. Thus Benedict exhorts us to spend even more time engaged in these during Lent than is usual for us. Lent is, after all, a time to remedy the negligences of other times and, we hope, to develop some practices that may become more habitual for us. Thus our monastic life will become a continuous Lent.

Benedict's fifth recommended practice is self-denial (*abstinentia*). I am reminded of his words in the Prologue about renouncing self-will (RB Prol. 3), which is also to renounce what *I* want or crave. Self-indulgence makes us self-centered. The *I* becomes the center of our life. Self-denial, the willingness to say no to ourselves, opens our minds and hearts to God and to others. Giving in to ourselves in ways that are not of God, in a manner that is excessive and unnecessary, distracts us from God and distances us from God. Benedict spells out what some of these are in RB 49.7: food, drink, sleep, talkativeness, and silliness. All are forms of self-indulgence and self-centeredness rather than the God-centeredness that the life of the monk is to be about.

At Tautra, we also have some practices of abstinence that we do as a community, such as having only bread and water for dinner on Ash Wednesday and Good Friday, as is prescribed in our Cistercian constitutions (28.A), and having soup and bread for dinner on Wednesdays as well as on Fridays (per the monastic fast, RB 41.6-7). These practices emphasize not only the communal nature of our search for God but also the support we give to and receive from one another in our desire for God.

This focus on God and immersion in God's love leads to a deep joy that no one can take from us (John 16:22). It will be a joy that can not only endure any unimaginable wrongs and injustices that we may experience, but even overcome them (RB 7.39). Benedict speaks of joy in relation to our Lenten ascetical practices; in fact, he goes so far as to say that joy should be the manner in which we engage in these practices. It is a joy that comes from the Holy Spirit (RB 49.6).

Benedict speaks of joy twice in the eight verses that comprise chapter 49. Lent is preeminently a season of joy. How can it not be when one is focused on and immersed in the experience of God's love and mercy? How can it not be when my heart is more and more in touch with the reality of the gift of eternal life that is mine now and that will come to fullness on the other side of the life I now know? In this spirit, we enter into Lent looking forward to holy Easter (RB 49.7)—not only the Easter of this year but the Easter at the end of our lives— with joy and spiritual desire.

The Color of Light

Sr. Sheryl Frances Chen, OCSO

Turning. March is the month of conversion, turning away from sin, turning toward life.

Sr. Gilchrist is one of the founders of MIDDIM, Monastic Interreligious Dialogue. The Vatican has commissioned Benedictines and Cistercians to engage in dialogue with contemplatives in other religions, though in practice this means mostly Buddhists and Muslim Sufis. When she was elected prioress at Tautra Mariakloster, she asked me to be the coordinator of the Scandinavian commission of MIDDIM. In 2011 we organized a dialogue with some Sami (an ethnic group of native Norwegians) friends in Kirkenes, one of the northernmost ports of Norway, from which a Hurtigruten coastal steamer departs every day to return to Bergen: turning from north to south. The Sami women we met are herders of reindeer, that is, caribou. They told us of their traditional life, which depends on this animal to provide not only meat but also clothes, shelter, and transport. Tove Lill told us that reindeer does are pregnant in March, with the calves nearing term. As a result, the herders are careful to be especially quiet around the reindeer during this late gestation period so as not to disturb the does. Tove Lill said that on March 25, the fetuses turn in their mother's wombs to be in the correct position to be born: turning toward the opening, turning toward the light. That information was very interesting for us for whom March 25, the solemnity of the Annunciation (to Mary, of the birth of Jesus), is the foundation day of our monastery. It was also the foundation day for the monks at the first Tautra Mariakloster, in 1207. We who witnessed the birth of a new foundation are well aware of all that needs to be in the right position for the baby to be born.

Sr. Ina had entered the Cistercian monastery in Laval, France, in 1974. In 1990 she obtained permission to return to Norway to see if there was interest in re-establishing Cistercian life there. During the Saint Olav feast days in 1991, she met Bishop Georg Müller, the Roman Catholic bishop of Trondheim, who expressed his interest in supporting a possible foundation in the Trondheim diocese. Eventually a support group was formed. Every evening at 6 p.m. they prayed for the fulfillment of the project, in union with Sr. Ina. At the first meeting, the six women of the support group each put a ten-kroner coin on the table—the equivalent of one American dollar. They were not sure what a support group was supposed to do, but they assumed that the new project would need some money. Sr. Ina also met journalist Hanne Berentzen, who herself became a Cistercian nun at Wrentham Abbey in the US in 1993.

During the Saint Olav feastdays in 1992, the then-mayor of Frosta, Jens Hagerup, contacted the support group and invited Sr. Ina to start Cistercian life in the house next to the ruins on Tautra. In the summer of 1993, Sr. Marjoe was sent from Mississippi Abbey in Iowa to help Sr. Ina. The following summer, however, in 1994, this experiment in Cistercian life on Tautra was ended, because Sr. Ina became seriously ill and had to return to France. It looked as though the dream would not be fulfilled.

Across the Atlantic, Our Lady of the Mississippi Abbey had increased in numbers sufficiently that the nuns had to decide whether to build an extension to their monastery or start a new one. Bishops all over the world invited Mother Gail to their dioceses, including Australia, Tunisia, and Tautra. Bishop Müller was eager to bring Cistercian nuns to the Trondheim diocese. Though the nuns tried to buy property in Småland, a family home became available on Tautra at the last minute. The bishop purchased the site, together with the neighboring field where the permanent monastery would be built, and

Mother Gail sent seven nuns to Tautra, including Sr. Ina from
Laval and Sr. Hanne-Maria from Wrentham, in February 1999.

For the opening Mass on March 25, 1999, the support group
rented a large tent. Two local police stood at attention wearing
white gloves, to welcome people as they arrived for the Mass.
The sisters noticed that the neighbors had their flags at full
mast and were told that "flagging" is a Norwegian tradition.
People raise their flags on national holidays and civic occasions
like voting day, and also on important community events like
birthdays, confirmations, and weddings. Since March 25 was
not a civic occasion, it meant the neighbors were flagging because they considered us part of the community!

After the Mass and reception, people started drifting away,
but there were enough people left at Vespers time for the
foundresses to pray Vespers together. Since there was not
enough room in our small chapel, the nuns took everyone to
nearby Logtun church on the Frosta peninsula, a beautiful
Romanesque stone church that predates the Cistercian monks
of the thirteenth century. As everyone walked in, their attention
was drawn to the altarpiece, from a hundred years after the
Reformation: it is of the Annunciation, and the only one in
Norway!

Mother Rosemary Durcan was named superior of the new
foundation. Under her leadership the nuns had to turn three
small family dwellings into a monastery. They began by establishing the most important rooms of a monastery: first the
chapel, then the refectory, chapter room, and scriptorium. Because they didn't yet have room for the scriptorium, they instead used their individual cells for spiritual reading. Some of
the cells had to have several functions, for example sewing,
wardrobe, liturgy office, and passageway.

Saint Benedict encourages nuns who live according to his
Rule to earn their living by the labor of their own hands. While
at Mississippi Abbey, Sr. Gilchrist had made herbal soap as a
hobby, so the nuns decided to try soap production as their main
industry. A room in one house was set aside as the soap factory.

Everything that had to do with the business had to be done there: research and development, purchasing ingredients, making the soap itself, cutting and storing it, wrapping and packing, shipping and billing. In 2001 when a benefactor made it possible to build an extension onto the red house, the addition housed three more cells and an extension of the soap factory on the ground floor.

We began to plan the future permanent monastery in 2000. For eighteen months they worked with architect Svein Skibnes until he had to resign. Although the nuns were disappointed by the delay, they interpreted it as a sign that God wanted to use the time to create the real monastery building: the community. To have to listen to one another and respect different viewpoints demands that the values of the Gospel be lived each day. Over this time the sisters discovered an underlying unity, which could mean only that the Holy Spirit was chiseling living stones, which together would form the new church on Tautra.

Just before Christmas 2002, architect Jan Olav Jensen began working on the plans for the new building. The nuns had to begin the whole process of dialogue again, explaining how a monastery is run, what the Rule demands, why the rooms had to be built a certain way, what values had to be preserved through the architecture. The total budget was 48.5 million kroner. See what multiplication the Lord did with those first 60 kroner laid on the table!

Although the church was not quite finished by the foundation date in 2006, on March 25 of that year the nuns celebrated the special ceremony that would make Tautra Mariakloster an independent monastery. Then six nuns—Sr. Rosemary, Sr. Marjoe, Sr. Lisbeth, Sr. Sheryl, Sr. Gilchrist, and Sr. Hanne-Maria—all changed their stability from their motherhouses in the US and promised to live with the community of Tautra Mariakloster the rest of their lives. The next day the community elected Sr. Rosemary as Tautra Mariakloster's first prioress, for a six-year term.

During the Cistercian general chapter of September 2011, we asked to be elevated to a Major Priory, with full autonomy and economic independence. The chapter voted its approval, and on March 25, 2012, Tautra Mariakloster was raised to the rank of Major Priory. The next day the community elected Sr. Gilchrist as prioress for a six-year term.

March 25, 2018, was Palm Sunday, so the election was postponed till Easter week. Sr. Brigitte was elected the third prioress of Tautra Mariakloster on April 5.

None of our history could have happened without a continual conversion: turning toward one another, turning toward the opening, the opportunity God laid open before us, turning toward the light, with the little insight one has, and going forward in great trust that God will lead us on this step and the next. There's a saying in Norwegian that the path comes into being as we walk it: *Veien blir til mens vi går den.* As the right foot comes down, the place where the left foot is supposed to go appears. We had to hone our skills in both listening and waiting. The process of birth takes its own time. It cannot be rushed. No one knows the exact day or the hour. The earth turns on its axis, and sometimes—especially on March 25—something special happens on Tautra.

The Space Between[1]

Silence could be described as "the space between"—when nothing happens. My father sent me a DVD of a TV program about the development of the Helvetica font. In my former life I was an editor, and I have always been interested in words and the art of printing. A font designer was interviewed on the DVD. He said that what made Helvetica such a great success was not the form of the letters themselves, but the space between them. When we read, we see not only the black letters,

---

[1] Some portions of this section of the chapter were originally published under my name in *U.S. Catholic* in March 2011. They are reprinted here by permission from *U.S. Catholic*.

but also the white space behind the letters, and the distance from one letter to the next. There is also the white space within the letters themselves, the relationship between one part of a letter and another part of itself. Helvetica is supremely readable because of both the positive and the negative, which taken together form a unity that is easy to understand.

And then there's music. What makes music beautiful is not the notes themselves, but what happens between them: the distance between the tones and the length of the pauses. All Western music is based on the same eight tones. What is ingenious about music is the way these tones are placed together and separated from one another. It is the silence between the tones that makes one piece of music different from another piece.

The Grand Canyon is incredibly beautiful because of the huge distance between its two sides. It's a miracle of nature. One can only stand open-mouthed on the edge of the canyon and stare across to the other side. Silence reigns. It is hardly possible to hear the Colorado River, 1.8 km down below, which has taken 6 million years to carve out the canyon. The canyon itself is 446 km long, and its breadth varies between 6.4 km— like from Tautra to the other side of the Trondheim Fjord—and 29 km. A viewer is struck dumb when trying to comprehend the size of that gorge.

I suggest that in the same way it is silence that makes life readable. Silence is the space between the letters of life. Silence contemplates both the positive and the negative together, to make a unit that maybe isn't exactly easy to understand but that makes life more comprehensible than if we never experience silence. When we get better at hearing the pauses in life, we discover a beautiful music that lies behind everything.

Sometimes we are struck dumb at the thought that we exist at all, and that we are only a few small creatures standing open-mouthed at the edge of God's amazing universe. Sr. Thea Bowman says, "I don't try to understand suffering; I try to understand life." Maybe what makes life understandable is not the events that happen, but what happens between them.

When I entered the monastery, the rule of silence was quite strict. We used a sign language in order to avoid speaking. There were seven rooms in the monastery where we could not speak at all—nor could we use the sign language in these places. Of course we observed the Great Silence, which begins after Compline and lasts until after Mass the next day. This rule of silence meant that I had to cross over a threshold. I had to leave the world I knew and enter another. I discovered a whole other space. When I could not speak with my novice mistress or the other novices, I had to learn to wait, and to tolerate the solitude. I had to learn to talk with God instead of other people. I discovered how much of our speech is really unnecessary. The discipline of silence changed my relationship with others, and with God. I had to take the things I was concerned about into my prayer. And many times I had to sit in silence and try to quiet the many thoughts in my head and listen to God—who has the habit of speaking in a very soft voice. The universe is incomprehensibly large, and it is over thirteen billion years old. From earth to the nearest star is four light years—it takes four years traveling at the speed of light to get there! From one end of the universe to the other is at least ninety-three billion light years! When I try to comprehend these numbers, my mind just can't grasp it. It means that even though the stars look uncountable, they can be counted. It means that there is a whole lot of space between them. Is it this space that makes the universe readable? Is it the space between that is God?

In the monastery we get up early, 4 a.m., and begin the day with Vigils. We have learned that it is best to use the early, quiet hours of the morning for prayer and *lectio*, before the workday starts getting hectic. During the day we try to speak only when necessary at work, to explain what needs to be done. This restraint creates an atmosphere that makes it easier to listen to God in one's heart. Silence is not only for me, but also for my sister, who is perhaps conversing with God in that moment.

We believe that God is worthy of worship, independent of our feelings. After I had made solemn profession, our community was helped by a psychologist to improve our dialogues. He pointed out that most of us treat others, and even God, as things to be used. Think about it for a moment. Don't we usually act as though our sister or our neighbor is someone we want to get something from? How often do we treat God as if he were a parking machine? I put in twenty kroner, and I get a slip of paper that gives me permission to park, or I get good weather, or good results on a test. The psychologist asked us to think of images of God that did not use him as a thing. The only image I could come up with was Jesus and me sitting on a park bench enjoying a beautiful sunset together. For me this is a picture of contemplative presence. Nothing is said. We enjoy each other and the sunset without words. We don't demand anything of the other. We communicate and are united without speaking. Perhaps a married couple who have grown old together develop this ability to communicate deeply in silence.

We had a retreatant who liked to go for walks in the bird sanctuary. She read the signs posted on the way to the bird observation tower: KEEP QUIET, STAY ON THE PATH. She took it as a mantra for that week, and maybe for life. KEEP QUIET, STAY ON THE PATH. KEEP QUIET, STAY ON THE PATH. KEEP QUIET, STAY ON THE PATH. Maybe it is only when we are silent that we can stay on the path of the Gospel.

A pilot told me once how he could find his way back to the airport if he got lost. Radio towers placed at certain intervals from the airport send out radio waves in the four directions: north, east, south, and west. The pilot tries to find one of these beams and to follow it back to the tower. Directly over the tower, there are no signals. When the pilot flies over the tower, there is a "pop" and then dead silence. For the first time, the pilot knows exactly where he or she is. It is an image for me: sometimes it is only in silence that we get to know ourselves. We sense the presence of God, and we try to come nearer, like following the radio waves on a straight path. We discover that we are home when we are in the center where it is absolutely silent.

When I was at my thirtieth reunion at Yale, I attended a lecture by a young psychologist using MRI to map cognitive areas of the brain. He showed a short video clip of two basketball teams, one wearing white and one wearing black. We were to count how many times the white team passed the ball to their own team. There were two different kinds of passes: a straight pass and a bounce pass. He said we had to concentrate on the task, and that it was best done in silence so we wouldn't distract others. So we did it, and he said the correct answer was twelve straight passes and two bounce passes. Then he asked, "Did you see the gorilla?" There must have been two hundred of us in the room, and no one knew what he was talking about. He showed the video again, but this time we didn't have to count. We saw a student dressed in a gorilla costume walk onto the scene while the teams were passing the ball. He even beat his chest and then walked off. We could not believe that we had not seen the gorilla!

I noticed that the professor had said to do the task in silence, as that would help us not to lose concentration. I took it as an image of what monastic life should be: if we keep silence and focus on Jesus, we won't see the gorillas who walk onto the scenes of our daily life. Often they are demanding, and they try to get our attention and get us off the path of what we should have done. And I noticed that the psychologist recommended silence not only for each of us, but so that others would not be distracted. Exactly as in the monastery!

When I returned here and told this story, one of our novices asked, "But the professor gave the directive to be silent. Who will do that for us?" I think the answer is *lectio divina*. It is Jesus himself who calls us to silence, to get to know him better.

I recently read a book on Jung's theory about how people grow psychologically. The author reminded the reader that growth in self-knowledge is a lifelong process. From day to day we see little progress, and the goal seems far away. Books about spiritual growth often describe the high points or signposts, for example Teresa of Avila's rooms in the interior castle or Benedict's twelve steps of humility. The books say little about the years of hard, necessary work that are needed to make real progress in any spiritual journey. I like the line in our Constitutions that describes Cistercian life as "ordinary, obscure and laborious." Between the chapters of the book of life, there is a lot of silence. And that's where God meets us.

Last summer we were visited by a German pilgrim who had walked a good deal of the trail to Nidaros cathedral. As she stood next to the final milestone, marked with the pilgrim's cross and "0 km to Nidaros," she said, she knew that she should feel relief and gratitude at reaching her goal. But instead, she felt a strong sense that her journey was not over. There was something else she was supposed to do. I was working at our booth, selling soap at the medieval market, and met her there; she asked if it was true we had a guesthouse, and could she come for a few days. I knew that that weekend the guesthouse was full, but I said that perhaps someone would be leaving on Monday, and she could come then. So on Monday she came to us. That day another guest happened to be there, a professional counselor, and she spent quite a lot of time with the pilgrim. The pilgrim finally left Tautra after some days, with some healing and some ideas for practical steps to get her life back in order. The counselor remarked that she had not expected to spend her retreat helping someone else, but she thought God had ordained it that way, and that she had been able to help her.

I reflected that this was so typical of the way God works. Here was a pilgrim standing next to the milestone that declared, "You've reached your goal!" but she hadn't. She needed some space between, some silence at the Tautra guesthouse, and some silence to listen to God in herself, before she could go on in peace toward the next milestone.

One year an abbess from the Netherlands gave us our retreat and framed the spiritual life as a pilgrimage. She read a poem that she translated from Dutch, and one line hit me: "I didn't know there were such huge trees between such tiny flowers." I think the huge trees are the events in our daily life that we are taken up with and sometimes swallowed up by, and the tiny beautiful flowers are the silence between them. I hope we take the time to discover the tiny flowers of life.

Though the proliferation of computers and the rapidity of cyberspace seem to have made instant gratification the norm, we still spend a lot of time waiting. We wait in line, we wait for results on an exam at school, or for the results of medical tests at the hospital, we wait for an answer to our query to come by email, or after a job interview for a letter to come in the post, we wait in a queue on the phone, we wait for the work week to be over. We wait for a gift we have long hoped to receive, we wait for a guest to show up, we wait for a friend or a significant relationship in our life, we wait for God's answer to our prayers. We wait for a certain date to arrive: a birthday or an anniversary or a special occasion, our own or others'. Has all this waiting made us more patient, or more impatient?

I recently read an essay about China in which a local man said he waits most for food and sleep. He can never count on getting enough of either, and the circumstances for the availability of both are entirely out of his control. Perhaps we who live in an affluent society with almost everything we could want readily available would do well to stop and ponder the millions of people who have no choice but to wait every day for the basics of life.

After Advent and Christmas, the second great liturgical season of the church is Lent-Easter-Pentecost. The forty days of Lent—usually all of March—are a spiritual preparation for the solemn remembrance of Jesus' suffering and death on Calvary, culminating in his bodily resurrection on the third day. The fifty days of Easter draw to a close as the church celebrates the Lord's ascension into heaven and the gift of the Holy Spirit at Pentecost. When we wait for a friend or a family member at the airport, what we see depends on whom we expect. There can be hundreds of other people on the same plane, but we peer into the crowd coming through the door and ignore everyone else, looking only for the one person we are waiting for. If it has been a long time since we have seen her, we may even feel our heart beating faster in excitement and anticipation. Will he look the same as when we last saw him? Will she be the same person we knew, or will her personality have changed over the intervening time of separation?

Lent can have this charge of excitement in the air as we prepare for Easter. We peer into the procession of days, looking for the one person we are waiting for: Jesus. In some privileged moments of prayer, we may even feel our heart beating faster in anticipation. Will I recognize him when he comes? Will he recognize me? Can I concentrate on seeing Jesus in the midst of the crowd of my busy, daily life?

Sometimes the waiting can't be rushed. As a pregnant woman has to wait until the proper time for her baby to be born, some things we wait for have to develop and mature. Once I was on retreat after I had come out of a difficult relationship. I longed to be able to forgive the other person, and—harder—to ask for forgiveness. I sensed that I had a lot of interior work to do and that the process could not be rushed. Forgiveness became the theme of my retreat, and I prayed a lot about it. I tried to open myself to receive God's healing, and toward the end of the week I felt moved to write a letter asking for forgiveness for the hurt we had caused each other. I felt great relief and new freedom as I sealed the envelope and posted it, and I knew that my baby of forgiveness could not have been brought to birth one moment earlier.

Our waiting can seem to be in vain. Perhaps we are waiting for the wrong thing, and so we don't recognize the answer when it comes. While waiting for email from God, we can discern signs of God's will through the fallible human beings God puts in our path. God uses our parents, our bosses at work, our religious superiors, our friends, and even our enemies to nudge us onto the path that opens before us. As the Dalai Lama says, sometimes our enemy can be our best teacher. When Jesus says to love our enemies, he's not just making a challenging statement; he's also psychologically accurate. We need to turn toward the opening, no matter how difficult or disguised the messenger.

March is one of Mary's months. I once heard a homily on a feast of Mary when the priest declared that he tried to do what Mary did: unless he had compelling reasons to say no, he always said yes. A little later, we received a letter from a lawyer who said that an army couple, both majors, who had no dependents, had willed their entire estate to us, and it would be nice if some sisters could come to their funeral. The superior asked Sr. Jane, who remembered the homily. She thought, "I don't have anything planned for Saturday afternoon," and said yes. It was a full military funeral, impressive as only the military knows how, not a dry eye when taps was played. Sr. Jane was even more moved than everyone else, because she had not been allowed to go home for her own father's funeral and still bore the grief. She came home from these unknown majors' funeral and declared with relief, "I think I just buried my father." All because she had said yes.

Our practices of silence are not the end of our monastic life. They are meant to open us up to God however he comes to us, especially in our sister who often doesn't look or act like Jesus. Scripture doesn't say what Mary was doing when the archangel Gabriel appeared. Maybe she was cooking dinner, and the angel was an interruption.

IF
she had not stilled her own soul
like a weaned child
on the breast of God
IF
she had not learned
to touch presence
in emptiness

IF
she had not attuned her inner ear
to the heartbeat of God
or the whirr of wings
Would she have even noticed the angel?

We live by faith, not by reason. So if a sister asks me to do something, it's not necessary that she explain her reasons. We are to set the other's best before our own. We are to become other-centered. We should immediately drop what we are doing to serve her.

Once I had to make a very deep and serious sacramental confession. The priest listened attentively and guided me with firm, even strict, counsel. I was grateful for the way he took me seriously, named sin for what it was, and pointed me in the right direction. At the end, after absolution, I was still kneeling and wanted, spontaneously, to kiss his hand in gratitude and respect for one who had so clearly mediated Jesus to me. I could feel him pull back, as if to say, "Don't do that, I'm only a human being." But then he dropped his own agenda and let me do it. I was so impressed. Here was someone who must be in the habit of letting go of his own preferences and preferring what the other wants. Otherwise he wouldn't have been able to do it so quickly. If we are really living the Gospel, putting the other first should become a habitual reaction.

Integration

Confessed, I stayed in grace, forgiven there.
Still kneeling, bent to kiss his ring in praise
Which absent from his finger showed malaise,
Disdain for mitred pomp, abbatial flair.
But can you take this gesture in and care
About my thanks? At once he dropped his ways,
Held fast my hand; I, trembling, met his gaze:

The eyes of Christ whose depth I could not bear.
So swift, so total and complete, the deed
Undoes the inward turn of Eden's goal
To shun the other, save one's own, and plead
Self-siege. Now outward flung, a glowing coal,
He stooped to center on the other's need.
One act of love, and I was seared, made whole.

We have the practice of not greeting one another during the great silence. During the day, however, when we pass one another in the hall, we give a smile even before we see who it is. We try not to allow ourselves to judge whether we like the person or not. We give a smile freely because Jesus is in her.

So I wonder, if an angel appeared to me, would I say
Sorry, I'm busy now, come back later
Don't disturb me during the great silence
Explain what you mean and I'll think about it
Can you send me an email and I'll look at it after dinner?

I found an Annunciation by Daniel Bonnell on the Internet. The wings look like huge ears, as if to say: Listen! God's word is here.

What do wings sound like? What is the sound of one wing clapping? The angel holds its hands in a way that reminds me of the laying on of hands at an ordination. Mary is to be ordained to bear the High Priest Jesus. Where was she going when the angel appeared? Was she just doing the daily routine, getting out of bed and going to church for Vigils?

I looked up feathers on the Internet. I discovered the Linneaus class for birds is Ave—as in avian, aviation, aviary! What did the angel say? Ave Maria! One of the functions of feathers is to capture air so the feathers insulate the bird—or the person who has a down quilt, as is common in Norway. The eider ducks on Tautra were famous for the quality of their down, and I bet more than one monk on medieval Tautra had a down pillow. These small pockets of air capture emptiness—which, together with the living creature, creates a warm presence.

I found another Annunciation by David Tanner, from 1898. The angel's presence is portrayed by light. Was Mary awakened at night? Or was it as if the sunrise were coming into her room? Did she see the light, or did she feel the presence? In the monastery we've been talking about the quality of our presence to one another. What does presence feel like? Was the presence of the angel comforting, or was it frightening? When we encounter one another, am I empty enough of my ego that my presence is a comfort to the other? Or am I filled with myself and my own agenda, or driven by a powerful emotion, so that my presence is perhaps instead frightening?

On one of my visits to my parents in Los Angeles, I went to the Getty Museum, where there was an exhibit on the use of blank space in paintings. What is the color of light? White light contains all the colors. It is only when light is split, as by a prism, that the rainbow emerges. Each drop of water acts as a prism to split the sunlight, resulting in the visible spectrum ROYGBIV. White light is a fullness of presence. Color is absence of some of the other wavelengths. How does a painter paint light? In that exhibit, the most common way was to leave blank the part that was to be light—so the white canvas showed through. The complete light was the emptiest space. The most intense presence was where human activity was most absent.

And finally I found a very modern Annunciation by British artist Gloria Ssali. At first I thought the angel was on the left, because of the pattern that looks like feathers. Something looks like a hand, as if ushering the Word into Mary's womb. Then I thought it was the angel on the right, approaching Mary and overshadowing her with its wings. The angel's mouth seems to be open, in greeting, or breathing the word that Mary hears and conceives. And light and fire seem to come from it. Maybe it's meant to be ambiguous. Our Lady and the Holy Spirit. What shall this be? May I have this dance?

I hope we can be the women who attune our inner ear to the heartbeat of God, who listen for the whirr of wings on the way to Vigils, who find presence in the most empty spaces, who dance to bring the Holy to birth.

We turn to the light that is always changing and always streaming down from parting clouds over Tautra. Ave, Maria! Ave, Our Lady of the safe island, Our Lady of the safe harbor, Our Lady of the safe womb, Our Lady of the safe enclosed space.

Liturgy for a Solemn Afternoon

Pale sun, too weak to warm,
Fell silently on the young owl sitting motionless in the
    desert gulch.
Once in a while, its eyes blinked.
Gazed upon, it showed no fear.
Human curiosity could not discern its interior sickness.
    Behold, adore.
    Hagios ischyros.

The hours wore on. Watchers came and went.
The air grew chill and darkness fell.
Did the owl thirst?
In the dusk, its eyes closed and its muscles stiffened.
It tumbled down the hill and lay still.
The wood of a thorn tree had stopped its fall.
At the abbey atop the mesa, a curtain fluttered.
    Behold, adore.
    Hagios athanatos.

Wind ruffled the light and splendour of its feathers,
and a gloved hand reached cautiously to lift the body.
Black talons, sharp as razors, curled in an empty grasp.
The scent of skunk revealed the victim of their final swoop:
The bird's last supper had been rabid.
A near-perfect creature, never would it glide again before
    dawn.
Serene in death, it was buried.
    Behold, adore.
    Eleison imas.

Sr. Sheryl Frances Chen, OCSO

Passing Over

Sr. Anne Elizabeth Sweet, OCSO

Winter lingers well into April at Tautra, as Lent does most often. Patches of snow rest on the barren ground even as tiny green shoots make their way out of dark soil into the light and warmth of the sun's rays. Winter is passing over into spring. The Passover of the Lord draws nigh.

> *If we walk in the light as he himself is in the light, we have fellowship with one another.* (1 John 1:7)

It is most often in April that holy Easter to which we have looked forward with joy and spiritual desire (RB 49.7) occurs. Although the Triduum does not begin until the Evening Mass of the Lord's Supper on Holy Thursday, our special communal celebration begins at our morning chapter. At this time, we have a special ceremony of reconciliation, during which we each acknowledge those behaviors and attitudes by which we have broken down the peace and unity of the community during the past year, and we ask forgiveness from our sisters. We exchange a sign of peace with one another as a symbol of our forgiveness and reconciliation, each of us greeting every other sister in the community.

Throughout his Rule, Benedict stresses that all the members should be at peace. Peace is to be sought and pursued (RB Prol. 17); discord of any kind is to be avoided (RB 65.7-11). Benedict warns his monks against giving "a false peace" (RB 4.25) and

53

instructs them "to make peace with one's adversary before the sun sets" (RB 4.73).[1]

It can be a surprise to discover that peace and unity are not necessarily givens in a community, something that we might easily assume will be the case or expect to find there. Rather, these are things that we must work to foster and preserve. What is a given in any community is that no one would choose of herself to live with every other person who is there. Rather, we have been gathered by the call of God in this particular community, as our Cistercian Constitutions point out (Const 5). Our Cistercian fathers spoke of our life in community as a *schola caritatis*, a school of love. How to love, at least as Christ taught us, is something we must learn and practice.

In addition to our very different personalities, most of us at Tautra have the challenge not only of living in a new culture and learning a new language, but of living with people from eight different nationalities with eight different mother tongues. Misunderstandings can and do easily arise, and offense is unknowingly given because of these cultural differences.

Benedict is well aware of the need to consciously foster and preserve unity and peace within the community, and he gives us numerous tools to use in doing so, as in chapter four of his Rule, the Tools of Good Works. On close examination, we discover that most of these are either taken directly from Scripture or are based on Scripture. Our monastic life—and stability in the community—is the "workshop" (RB 4.78) in which we use these tools to co-create, in partnership with the Spirit of God, the person in God's likeness we were created to be. We need the support, the example, the help and challenge from one another in so becoming.

Our Cistercian fathers often use Saint Paul's words in Galatians 4:19 in speaking of the goal of our monastic *conversatio*:

---

[1] Leonard J. Doyle, trans., *The Rule of Saint Benedict* (Collegeville, MN: Liturgical Press, 1948), 2001. RB verse references are cited from RB 1980, ed. and trans. Timothy Fry (Collegeville, MN: Liturgical Press, 1981).

that Christ be formed in us. We were created or formed in the image of God, then deformed through sin. We need to be re-formed through conversion and transformed as we are more and more formed in Christ. This is the essence of the monastic *conversatio* we have vowed.

Our Holy Thursday reconciliation service is a time to ask forgiveness for the ways our own sin and self-centeredness deform our life together. We pray that our Lenten observances have transformed us. We enter into the Paschal celebration of the death and resurrection of Christ, whose life we share, rec-ognizing that the power that raised him from the dead is now at work in us (see Eph 1:19-20). We recommit ourselves to becoming together who we are called to be as the Body of Christ, blessed, broken, and given for one another. We enter into the Triduum knowing that the way of Jesus' passing over is to be our own.

Mass of the Lord's Supper

We should glory in the cross of Our Lord Jesus Christ,
in whom is our salvation, life and resurrection, through
whom we are saved and delivered. (Entrance antiphon,
Holy Thursday)

So begins our solemn celebration of the Sacred Triduum, those three days in which we re-member and re-live those last days of Jesus' life, when his total gift of self to the Father and to believers in every age was accomplished. These are the most sacred days of the year for us, and among the most moving of our liturgies. We are happy to share the experience of them with our retreatants and guests—our guesthouse is booked for these days long in advance. Friends and neighbors also join us for some of our services.

The evening service begins on a note of joy as voices, organ, and pealing church bells sing glory to the God who has deliv-ered his people from slavery. The first reading of the Mass recounts this event as experienced by the Israelites in Egypt (Exod 12:1-14). Its story has been passed on by the Jewish people and commemorated with a special meal continuously through the ages, down to and including our own time.

Each of the four gospels situates the suffering and death of Jesus at the time of the Passover. In the synoptic gospels, Jesus' last supper with his disciples is this Passover meal. In the gospel of John, Jesus' last meal with them is before the Passover, as Jesus dies at the hour when the lambs for the Passover meal were sacrificed. In either case the point is clear: Jesus' suffering and death inaugurated a new Passover, one that has been continuously commemorated down to our own day in the celebration of the Eucharist.

The earliest biblical account of the Eucharist is found in Paul's first letter to the Corinthians; it is the second reading of today's Mass (1 Cor 11:23-26). The context of Paul's account appears in verses 17 to 22 and 27 to 34. Here Paul takes issue with the way the Corinthians are celebrating the Eucharist, not on the basis of ritual concerns, but because of the "divisions" and "factions" that are manifest when they come together as church (vv. 18-19). The Eucharist is meant to be a communion with the blood of Christ, as today's responsorial antiphon, also from 1 Corinthians (10:16), makes clear. Our sharing of the bread and the cup, the Body and Blood of the Lord, is meant to be a communion with one another as well: "we who are many are one body, for we all partake of the one bread" (1 Cor 10:17).

Today's gospel is not an account of the institution of the Eucharist, but rather the model of service that Jesus enacted at the Last Supper when he washed the feet of his disciples, the job of a servant (John 13:1-15). It is both a model and a command of what we must be and do for one another: "I have set you an example, that you also should do as I have done to you. . . . I give you a new commandment, that you love one another. Just as I have loved you, you also should love one another" (John 13:15, 34). After the gospel reading, our prioress, who Benedict says holds the place of Christ in the community, washes our feet. (Benedict says that it is the abbot who holds the place of Christ [RB 2.2], but we are too small a community to have an abbess. Instead, it is the prioress who is the major superior.)

At Tautra, we have the custom of continuing the reading from chapter 13 of John's gospel after Communion, beginning with verse 33 and continuing up to and including John 14:31: "Rise, let us be on our way." Rising, we go in procession from the church to the chapter room, where we have the altar of repose. "Stay awake and pray" (Matt 26:41), and so we do.

After the evening Mass of Holy Thursday, neither the church bells nor the organ will be heard again until the Gloria of the Easter Vigil. We hear instead a wooden clapper calling us to prayer. The tone of these days is somber, marked as they are by betrayal, abandonment, intense anguish, and suffering. It is the hour of darkness.

Good Friday

Out of his anguish he shall see light. (Isa 53:11)

We enter into a dark and empty church for the celebration of Vigils. The tabernacle door is open; the icon of Our Lady has been removed from the sanctuary. We kneel in darkness as the prioress prays, "Lord Jesus, this is the day of your longest suffering and greatest pain, the day of your deep anxiety in soul and body. Make our hearts vigilant as we watch with you and keep alive in us the truth that love is the deepest meaning of it all. This we pray, O Savior of the world. . . ."

After a few minutes of silent prayer, the lights are turned on, and Vigils continues with the three psalms of the first nocturn. The Scripture reading is sung from the Lamentations of the prophet Jeremiah, mournful prayers over the destruction of Jerusalem in the wake of the Babylonian conquest of the city. Today we mourn Jesus, seized by the powers of darkness and put to death. A small group of sisters sings "Ave Verum" after the reading of the second Nocturn. At its conclusion, we kneel in prayer as the prioress prays, "Lord Jesus, we have watched with you this little while. May the memory of your bitter suffering and death remain in our hearts and bring us to an ever deeper understanding of your love for us. May your love strengthen our own wavering love, so that we increasingly grow in obedience and willing service. May all in our life, work, prayer, and suffering happen for the whole world you lived, prayed, and suffered for. Fulfill our growth in you so that your kingdom comes in all its fullness. This we pray in your name, Lord Jesus, the Savior of the world."

After Vigils, there is time for quiet prayer and *lectio* as usual. On other days throughout the year, we have Adoration of the Blessed Sacrament after Vigils, but not, of course, on Good Friday and Holy Saturday. I find that it is good to pray in the empty church. One can feel the absence of the Blessed Sacrament, just as the Presence can be felt at other times—as even our guests attest. On Good Friday and Holy Saturday, however, the emptiness is a stark reminder of the reality we are commemorating. It is good for us to enter into it so palpably.

We begin Lauds and all of the Offices on these days kneeling in quiet prayer together. On Good Friday, we conclude by kneeling and reciting Psalm 51: "Have mercy on me, O God, according to your steadfast love; according to your abundant mercy blot out my transgressions" (Ps 51:1). Today we come face to face with the death-dealing consequences of sin. We call on the Lord's steadfast love and abundant mercy (Exod 34:6; Ps 145:8).

Good Friday is a day of silence and of fasting for us. We know that we are sinners. We have chosen the way of darkness and death. In accord with our Cistercian constitutions, we have only bread and water for dinner. At Tautra, we also have only bread and water for breakfast. We have a simple casserole for the evening meal.

The service commemorating the Lord's passion begins at 3, the hour when Jesus died (Mark 15:33-37). For me, it is the most moving of all of our liturgies. The service opens in silence as the priest prostrates before the altar and the community and guests kneel.

The first reading is the fourth song of the Suffering Servant, Isaiah 52:13–53:12. We've heard the others proclaimed on Palm Sunday and the first three days of Holy Week (Isa 50:4-7; 42:1-7; 49:1-6). It is easy to see why the evangelists used this text to describe the suffering of Jesus, whose role as servant was highlighted in last evening's gospel. Biblical scholars are divided as to whether Isaiah's servant was a single individual, perhaps even the prophet himself, or the nation of Israel as a whole. A case can be made for both. Does this not suggest that we should hear this Word of the Lord not only with reference to Jesus but also to ourselves? Both as individuals and as church?

God's Word challenges us to examine ourselves: Are we the servants of the Lord that we have been called to become? Are we willing to pour ourselves out in death, in all the dyings that the gift of total self requires? Are we willing to enter into the darkness of suffering in body and in spirit? Can we do so with trust?

Today's responsorial antiphon shows us the way. It is the prayer of Jesus as he dies: "Father, into your hands I commend my spirit" (Luke 23:46). It can well be the prayer of all of us as we stand at the threshold of darkness, or even in its midst, whatever shape that darkness might take at a particular time. The verses chosen from responsorial Psalm 31, chosen for today, focus on the suffering experienced from foes and even neighbors and friends (Ps 31:2, 6, 12-13, 15-16, 17, 25). If we consider the psalm as a whole, we hear vivid descriptions of the suffering experienced as well as repeated prayers of trust. In writing these words, the psalmist's faith and trust is not only expressed, but continually formed and deepened. And so it can be with us when we pray these words.

The second reading from Hebrews first highlights the humanity of Jesus: "In the days of his flesh"—one of us, like us, knowing anguish and pain (Heb 4:14-16; 5:7-9). Every time I hear this reading, I am struck by what is always an enigma to me: "Jesus offered up prayers and supplications, with loud cries and tears, to the one who was able to save him from death, and he was heard because of his reverent submission." How could he have been heard when he died? He wasn't saved from death, he endured it. And that is precisely the point. In so doing, "he learned obedience through what he suffered" and was "made perfect." In other words, Jesus was saved from a death not of his own making precisely because he willingly entered into it.

Is this not the message of Benedict's fourth degree of humility, which gives us a handle on how to endure the difficult, unjust, and even injurious things not of our own making in our monastic lives (see RB 7.35-43)? Jesus was saved by the power of the Father, who raised him from the dead and brought him into a new, glorious, and transformed life. Thus, brought to completion and fullness of life, he is "perfected." The biblical sense of the word *perfect* implies "having matured," that is, having become what he was called to be. It is the "It is finished" of today's gospel (John 19:30). Jesus thus becomes "the source of eternal salvation for all who obey him" (Heb 5:9).

Jesus obeyed the Father and was brought through death to the glory of new life. So also will we be brought to life—and to God—through obedience: to God, to our prioress, and to one another. The call to obedience resounds throughout the Rule from beginning to end: "by the labor of obedience . . . return to Him from whom you had departed by the sloth of disobedience" (RB Prol. 2); "Not only is . . . obedience to be shown by all to the Abbot, but the brethren are also to obey one another, knowing that by this road of obedience they are going to God" (RB 71.1-2). In addition, all of chapters 5, 68, and 71 of the Rule pertain to obedience. For us, as for Jesus, obedience is the way to God and to life in all its fullness.

The gospel reading on Good Friday is always the passion narrative according to John. The fourth evangelist's account is quite different from that of the synoptics. Jesus manifests a noble dignity throughout the last days of his life. While there is no account of an agony in the garden in John, Jesus is troubled at the realization that his hour has come. Nonetheless, he prays, "What should I say—'Father, save me from this hour'? No, it is for this reason that I have come to this hour. Father, glorify your name" (John 12:27-28). And that glorification happens when Jesus is crucified. In John the moment of Jesus' "lifting up" on the cross is also the time of his exaltation in glory (John 3:14; 8:28; 12:32-33).

When the passion is read during the service, we prostrate at the words "He bowed his head and gave up his spirit" (John 19:30). We adore you, Christ, who by your cross, your perfect obedience to the Father, has redeemed the world.

The General Intercessions, embracing all God's people, conclude the Liturgy of the Word. We pray for the Church, for the Holy Father, for priests and deacons, for all the faithful, for catechumens preparing for baptism, for Christian unity, for the Jewish people, for those who do not believe in Christ, for those who do not believe in God, and for all who are suffering any tribulation.

The veneration of the cross follows the Intercessions. The celebrant comes from the back of the church carrying a simple wooden cross, made from wood from our own property: "Behold the wood of the Cross on which hung the salvation of the world." The chantresses sing the Reproaches in a plaintive harmony: "My people, what have I done to you or in what have I abandoned you?" The account of all that God had done in Israel's history and its failures to respond can easily be transcribed to our own story. It is we who have been unfaithful, in little and not so little ways, to God and to one another.

So we venerate the cross in repentance and adoration, prostrating three times: at the back of the choir stalls kneeling and bowing forward on our knuckles, in the middle of the choir stalls with a full prostration, and before the altar, kneeling to kiss the cross. It is truly a liturgical movement as the three sisters coordinate their going down in a prostration and rising up in order to move to the next station.

I am always moved to tears during this part of the ceremony, especially when the elderly and not so physically fit do each of the prostrations: sisters and guests, the old and the young, some in cowls, some in jeans. Here we are, the one body following the way of the One who is our head, knowing that his way must be our own.

The Good Friday service concludes with the rite of Holy Communion. We partake of the Body of Christ, the bread of the life given for us, and pray that we may have strength for our journey through death to life. We pray with Benedict that the Lord will "bring us all together to life everlasting" (RB 72.12).

Vespers is not celebrated on Good Friday. At the end of Compline, as on Holy Thursday, there is no blessing with Holy Water at the end of the service. We await the living waters of the glorified Jesus on Easter.

Holy Saturday

The Light shines in the darkness, and the darkness did not overcome it. (John 1:5)

Vigils begin as we kneel in the darkness of the church. The prioress prays, "Lord Jesus, your church watches tonight gathered around your tomb. The earth held your body but you were already visiting the places of darkness in the kingdom of death, bringing the fullness of your redeeming love, which you poured out on Good Friday, to all the dead who thirsted for your light. Christ our King, grant that we may grow in love and understanding as we honor your bitter suffering, your blessed death by crucifixion, and your burial, until our lives receive a share in your death and our death receive a share in your life. This we pray in your name, Savior of the world."

Once again, the first nocturn reading is from the Lamentations of Jeremiah, sung to a plaintive melody by a soloist. And as yesterday, a hymn follows the second nocturn reading. We kneel for the concluding prayer of Vigils: "Immortal Lord

Christ, you gave yourself into the power of death, so that through your suffering, death, and burial, you could save us from the destruction of death. Those who waited for your coming in the darkness of the kingdom of death saw the light of your glory even as you lay lifeless in the grave. Grant us also to see a glimpse of your great glory, so we can praise you for your loving mercy, you, humankind's friend . . . ."

As we did yesterday, we begin all the Offices of the day kneeling in quiet prayer. We conclude Lauds and Vespers kneeling and praying Psalm 51.

There is no Eucharist today. There is a felt emptiness in both the church and the monastery. The tabernacle is empty. The house is quiet. Nevertheless, as the day progresses, one can also sense the building up of an anticipation and even excitement in the house. The wood for the Paschal fire is ready by the cloister garden. The organist is practicing. One hears the Exultet being practiced behind closed doors. Flowers are prepared, the tables are set. All is in readiness. It is the Passover of the Lord.

Our Easter Vigil begins around three in the morning when we gather in the totally dark cloister around the rose garden. And so the presider begins: "On this most sacred night, in which our Lord Jesus Christ passed over from death to life, the Church calls upon her sons and daughters, scattered throughout the world, to come together to watch and pray. If we keep the memorial of the Lord's paschal solemnity in this way, listening to his word and celebrating his mysteries, then we shall have the sure hope of sharing his triumph over death and living with him in God."

Words that we hear year after year, but ever new. This, today, right now, is the Passover of the Lord and our own as well, from the darkness into light. The fire is kindled, at first but a glimmer, soon becoming sparks shooting through the wood, the acolyte breathes on them—reminiscent of God's breathing life into the lump of clay that became the first human being? And then the blaze: "O God, who through your Son bestowed upon the faithful the fire of your glory, sanctify this new fire, we pray, and grant that . . . we may be so inflamed with heavenly desires . . . ."

The candle is brought forth to be readied to bear the Light of Christ, Alpha and Omega, the beginning and the end, yesterday and today, right now, in this year, in this moment. Lumen Christi! Once we were in darkness, but now we are in the Light of the Lord! The Light spreads through the darkness as we make our way to the church. There the exultant hymn of praise is sung before the Easter Candle, "a pillar of fire" glowing to the honor of God, symbolizing the Risen Christ, who has conquered the darkness of death.

At Tautra, we have all seven Old Testament readings and responses during the Liturgy of the Word, and I would not want to omit a single one! The stories of creation and of Israel are *our* stories, not only because we are spiritual descendants of Abraham but because these stories unfold in our own lives as well. We, too, experience creation and re-creation (Gen 1:1–2:2), we too know the promises of the Lord and, at times, the heart-wrenching sacrifices that are asked (Gen 22:1-18). There have been times when we, too, have felt enslavement and the liberation that could come only through a miraculous deed of the Lord (Exod 14:15–15:1). Our Creator has entered into covenant with us as well as with Israel of old and become our spouse in intimate knowledge and love (Isa 54:5-14). We too are invited to come to the true living water that only the Lord can offer us (Isa 55:1-11). We too are reminded that "what is pleasing to God is known to us" (Bar 3:9-15, 32–4:4). We too are purified as the Lord sprinkles clean water upon us and gives us a new heart and a new spirit (see Ezek 36:16-28).

"Glory to God in the highest!" The organ bursts forth, the bells peal. Glory to God in the highest and to you, Lord Jesus, who takes away the sins of the world. Paul's words to the Romans makes it clear that this salvation is ours through baptism: "Do you not know that all of us who were baptized into Christ Jesus were baptized into his death . . . so that, just as Christ was raised from the dead, . . . we too might walk in newness of life?" (Rom 6:3-11). Alleluia! Alleluia! Alleluia! For the first time in forty days we hear that glorious word. Alleluia! Alleluia! Alleluia! praise the Lord. We hear the story of that first Easter morning when those faithful women disciples went to the now-empty tomb of Jesus (Matt 28:1-10; Mark 16:1-7; Luke 24:1-12). "He is not here." "He has been raised." "He goes before you." Alleluia!

He goes before us. His way through death into newness of life must be our own. We recommit ourselves to the promises made for us at baptism and are blessed with the new and living water of Easter.

Several times over the years we at Tautra have had the joy of a friend of the community or a volunteer making profession of faith during the Easter Vigil and so becoming fully initiated into the Roman Catholic Church. We are not about proselytizing, but it is a joy for us when our friends find their home in the Catholic Church and we can share the Eucharist together. We pray for that day when all Christians can share in the bread and the cup of the Lord.

Our Easter Vigil concludes—and our Easter celebration begins—just as the sun rises on the horizon and fills our church with light. "This is the day that the Lord has made; let us rejoice and be glad in it!" (Ps 118:24).

The community shares breakfast after the Easter Vigil with our guests and friends who have joined us for the Vigil. It is a special time for all. Many join us for the celebration of Lauds that soon follows. Alleluia! This is the day the Lord has made!

There is a specialness about the church on Easter Sunday, more so perhaps than on any other day in the year. The smell of incense lingers in the air; our Easter candle burns brightly at the side of the altar, as do our own candles from the Vigil; flowers, so long absent during the winter of Lent, adorn the altar and ambo. And we are there in church for most of the day! An hour of Adoration follows Lauds, then Tierce a short time later. Afterwards, everyone goes to the kitchen to help prepare a special Easter dinner before coming back to the church for Sext. None follows Easter dinner, and then, finally, a long-awaited meridian or rest. Vespers in the evening concludes the

Paschal Triduum. Our paschal celebration continues—first for the Octave: seven more days of solemnities celebrating the great feast—up to and including Pentecost some fifty days later.

April Feasts

Blessed Maria Gabriella Sagheddu: April 22 (1914–1939)

"That they may be one" (John 17:11) . . . *in the Light of the Lord.*

Blessed Maria Gabriella (1914–1939) was an Italian Cistercian nun at the monastery of Grottaferrata (now Vitorchiano). Under the influence of her Abbess Mother Maria Pia Gullini, a love and devotion to the cause of Christian Unity was fostered in Gabriella's heart. This was far in advance of the impetus it now has today after the attention given to it by the Second Vatican Council (the Document on Ecumenism). Gabriella wished to offer her life in prayer and sacrifice for this cause. On the day she made her offering of self as a sacrifice, she was stricken with tuberculosis, and she died some fifteen months later. It was the fourth Sunday of Easter, "Good Shepherd" Sunday, with its gospel from John 10. She had been in monastic life for three and a half years.

Gabriella's devotion to the cause of Christian Unity is something that we at Tautra share. Catholics are a minority in Norway, as most Norwegians are Lutherans. We have many Lutheran guests on retreat and count among our friends several Lutheran bishops and priests. We participate in the local ecumenical prayer services during the Week of Prayer for Christian Unity and host the annual Women's Day of Prayer each March. At times, Lutheran services have been held in our church.

My experience at Tautra is that Christian Unity is not something that is talked about once a year, but something that is lived throughout the year. The image that is uppermost in my mind has to do with the celebration of the Eucharist. We are pained that we cannot share the Eucharist with our Lutheran friends. Our practice, when we are in one another's churches for a service, is at the time of Communion to come forward with our right hand on our left shoulder, a sign that we are asking for a blessing rather than to receive. Once, at the dedication of the new church of the Brigittine Sisters in Trondheim, I watched as the Lutheran bishop came forward at the time of Communion to the Catholic Bishop-Presider and asked for a blessing. After blessing his Lutheran brother, the Catholic bishop asked for his blessing. The image spoke volumes to me, and I have never forgotten it.

In addition to her devotion to the cause of Christian Unity, Gabriella became significant to me personally at the time of my mother's last illness, which came suddenly and unexpectedly. When I received word of it, she was on a respirator in intensive care and not responsive. I flew to the States as soon as possible, hoping that I would see her before she died. When I arrived, I was told that her doctor wanted to talk with me about taking her off the respirator. To this day, I do not remember his name, other than that it sounded like Sagheddu. I kept saying Dr. Sagheddu only quickly to remind myself that that was Gabriella's last name, not his. Finally, it dawned on me, if Gabriella is so much on my mind, maybe there is a reason, maybe I should pray to her.

It took some days before my brother and I were willing to remove the respirator. The doctor had not been hopeful when I kept saying to leave her on it, perhaps she would become conscious again. So, after some days, we agreed. As it turned out, my mother did not die when the respirator was removed. We were told, however, that she could not remain in the hospital more than five days. Medicare rules, I suppose.

We moved my mother to a care center run by the Sisters of Mercy. On the second day there, two of my cousins came and wanted to talk with me. They were of the strong opinion that I should not go to Iowa, where I was scheduled to teach for a week in a program for our temporary professed monks and nuns, nor return to Norway. Rather, my cousins thought that I should stay in Mobile and care for my mother. This put me into a real dilemma. Of course I wanted to care for my mother. However, the doctor had also told us that since she continued to live after being taken off the respirator, her condition—still non-responsive—could go on for years.

Shortly after my cousins left, the nurses came to turn my mother. I went out to the courtyard outside her room, sat down, and prayed to Blessed Gabriella, whose name had been so much on my mind. "What should I do?" "Please let me know." Shortly afterwards, back in my mother's room, I noticed that her breathing had changed. I called the family and the chaplain to come. An hour or so later, while we were all gathered around her bed, praying aloud and talking to her, my mother slipped away in a very peaceful death.

It was hard, all so unexpected, happening within the space of a month. But my mother, who had worked full time as an accountant until the age of eighty and was forced to retire when the business was bought out and her job didn't carry over, and who had found retirement so difficult, was at last at peace at the age of eighty-three. I attribute her peaceful death, which resolved my own dilemma, to Blessed Gabriella's intercession. We are so pleased to have a relic of Blessed Gabriella in the altar of our church; it is especially meaningful to me.

Saint Mark: April 25

And very early on the first day of the week, when the sun had risen, they went to the tomb. (Mark 16:2)

How fitting to celebrate the feast of Saint Mark during the Easter season, since it was Mark who was the first to compose a gospel, putting Jesus' teachings and the stories about him that had been circulating in the oral tradition into a narrative format. Mark's focus was twofold: Christology and discipleship. "Who do you say that I am?" as Jesus asked his first followers, and "What must I do to be a disciple of Jesus?" The answers to both questions are clear. Jesus is the Christ, the Son of God (Mark 1:1). Those who would be his disciples must be willing to follow his "way" (a favorite image in the gospel) even to the point of death. "Are you able to drink the cup that I drink, or be baptized with the baptism that I am baptized with?" (Mark 10:38). "There is no one who has left house or brothers or sisters or mother or father or children or fields for my sake and for the sake of the good news who will not receive a hundredfold now in this age—houses, brothers and sisters, mothers and children, and fields, with persecutions—and in the age to come eternal life" (Mark 10:29-30). Mark's mention of persecution here is unique to him among the gospels. It is a reality that reflects the life situation of the community for whom Mark wrote, a community undergoing suffering because of their Christian commitment.

Yet another aspect of discipleship is particularly relevant for disciples after Jesus' resurrection. Mark alone of the four evangelists does not recount an appearance of the Risen Lord. Most biblical scholars are in agreement that Mark's gospel originally ended with 16:8. Subsequent verses were added later by those who were perhaps uncomfortable with this ending and who summarized the appearance narratives from other gospels.

In verse 8, the women fled from the empty tomb in fear and amazement, and because of that fear said nothing about what they had seen and heard. The reader, however, has also heard the message and knows that Jesus has been raised and that he goes ahead of the disciples to Galilee. The reader knows that "there [they] will see him" (Mark 16:7).

Is this not the reality with which we all must live? Jesus has been raised. He goes before us. One day we shall see him in his risen glory. In the meantime, we must live with the message and the promise. Blessed are we who have not seen, and yet believe.

And so we go forward, following his way . . . .

Saint Rafael Arnáiz Barón (1911–1938): April 27

Rafael is one of the more recently canonized saints of our Order (2009), and thus it is fitting to speak of him here. Having died in 1938, he is perhaps not as well known as other saints. I myself met him for the first time, one might say, when writing this chapter. The encounter has been a blessing for me. His words and his example have spoken deeply to me in my own life experience. Rafael was a man who learned how to adapt peacefully to the circumstances of his life that were beyond his control and that impacted his life, his hopes, and his dreams in such a profound way that on at least several occasions, it seemed impossible that they could be fulfilled.

It is no surprise that Saint Pope John Paul II named Saint Rafael as one of the patrons of the World Youth Day in Madrid in 2011. This young Spanish monk was but twenty-seven years old when he died.

Born to a deeply religious Spanish family, Rafael learned to know and love the Lord at a very early age, and his faith was nurtured by the Lord's grace as well as by the example and witness of his family. Their material wealth provided Rafael with many opportunities, a Jesuit education and architectural studies not least among them. Rafael was naturally quite talented, especially in art. He enjoyed the good life he experienced with his family as well as with his peers. At the same time he maintained his fidelity to the practice of prayer, which at one point in his studies included daily Mass, rosary, and thirty minutes of prayer before the Blessed Sacrament.

Gradually, Rafael heard within himself a call to monastic life and entered the monastery of San Isidoro (now Isidro) in 1934 at the age of twenty-three. What is unique about Rafael's monastic journey is that he entered four times in the space of four and a half years, his departures necessitated by the gravity of his diabetic illness, military conscription, and the political situation in his country at the time of the Spanish Civil War. When both the condition of his health and the political situation were such that he could return to the monastery, he did so as an oblate, since the rigors of monastic life were too much for him.

Particularly moving in Rafael's story, as revealed in his reflective writings and letters, are his accounts of his struggles in trying to understand the ways of God in his life. At times he experienced much darkness and desolation, but always, eventually, much light: "God is good and kind; he parts a veil, and in my darkness I see Jesus—sweet, calm, he shows me his wounds, he shows me how much he loved the world, how much he loves me."[2] Sometimes the light came through "a good thought, a word read by chance in a book . . . a phrase of the Gospel is enough to dispel my darkness and fill my soul with light."[3]

God's light sharpened Rafael's focus as he was led through a growing sense of detachment from all that he held dear: family, lifestyle, studies, even his own desire to be a monk, which his illness rendered impossible. Detached from all, Rafael was free to focus on "God alone."

" 'Lord, Lord' . . . 'as the deer longs for running streams,' as the doe sniffs the air seeking that with which to slake its thirst, so my soul thirsts for life . . . life eternal; a life of space and light, a life in which that tiny candelabra within will swell and burst into flame, and at the sight of your face will shine brighter than the sun."[4]

Rafael is an inspiration for anyone who must adapt to circumstances in life not of their own choosing—for Rafael, his diabetes—which alter their hopes and plans, even rendering

[2] M. Rafael Barón, "Life and Writings of Brother M. Rafael Barón (IV–V)," trans. Mary Charles Longuemare, CSQ 36, no. 1 (2001): 41–84, here 81; *Vida y Escritos de Fray Maria Rafael Arnáiz Barón*, ed. Damian Yáñez, 11th ed., Venta de Baños, Palencia: San Isidro de Dueñas (Madrid: PS Editorial, Covarrubia, 1974).

[3] M. Rafael Barón, "Life and Writings of Rafael Arnáiz Barón (VII)," trans. Mary Charles Longuemare, CSQ 38, no. 1 (2003): 35–83, here 46.

[4] M. Rafael Barón, "Life and Writings of Brother M. Rafael Barón (III)," trans. Juanita Colon, CSQ 35, no. 1 (2000): 77–92, here 80.

them unattainable. And who among us has not felt the impact of circumstances beyond our control, even if less dramatic than Rafael experienced. Rafael shows us the way through the seemingly devastating losses. By focusing on "God alone," Rafael discovered that in God he had all. So can we: "it all consists in knowing how to wait, and in the end, when life is over, our soul will quench its thirst at the one and only fountain, which is God."[5]

Saint Catherine of Siena: April 29 (1347–1380)

Those who are wise shall shine like the brightness of the sky, and those who lead many to righteousness, like the stars forever and ever. (Dan 12:3)

April draws to a close with the feast of Catherine of Siena, another patron saint of Europe. Catherine was a laywoman who became a third-order Dominican at the age of eighteen. For three years she lived in seclusion as she devoted herself to prayer and ascetical practices. The fruits of this period led to her more public ministry and involvement. Her reputation for holiness drew a number of followers or disciples. Catherine's spiritual teachings, rooted in the experience of prayer, are to be found in her book *The Dialogue*, written in the form of a conversation between herself and God. She is one of four women accorded the title Doctor of the Church.

Catherine, like the women in Mark's gospel who accompanied Jesus from Galilee to Jerusalem, followed his way to the cross as it took shape in her own life. For her, it meant meeting with opposition and misunderstanding, slander and suspicion. Like Gabriella's, Catherine's life was short; she died at the age of thirty-three. Like Gabriella, Catherine was passionate about church unity, only for her it was a matter of unity *within* the Roman Church. At one point in her life, there were actually

---

[5] Barón, "Life and Writings (III)," 80.

three popes—all claiming to be the real one! She worked tirelessly to bring an end to this division that unity might be restored to the church.

As we celebrate Catherine's feast at Tautra, we remember our Dominican Sisters at Lunden Kloster and Katarinahjemmet in Oslo, who have been so good to us from the very beginning of our plans for our foundation. We are so very grateful for their friendship, assistance, and hospitality through the years. We see in them Catherine's spirit of contemplation and deep love for the church and her tireless efforts for its unity and growth. As we celebrate Catherine's feast today, we ask her special intercession for our beloved sisters and for all of Europe for whom she is patron.

As April unfolds into May, those tiny green shoots have grown and bear buds that will soon flower. May it so be with us in our new life with the Risen Christ as we await the coming of the Spirit at Pentecost.

Perfect Day

Sr. Maria Rafael Bartlett, OCSO

Having just written the chapter for December during the winter, now, in March, writing about May is evocative for me. It's like a warm breeze carrying the scent of new growth: fresh spring leaves, slim green shoots, first blossoms appearing after the long winter. I lived much of my life in England, where May feels like a prelude to summer. Here on the island of Tautra, which is more temperate than many other inland or northern parts of Norway, May is when spring first becomes visible, tangible—when winter's longing for green at last starts to bear fruit. In the fertile agricultural region of Frosta, which adjoins our causeway across the fjord, it is considered to be spring as soon as the thawed ground can first begin to be dug for sowing, which is generally in April. For me, though, I remain reluctant to apply the word *spring* until I can see leaves on the trees—in May. Yet, although May here is when the trees first become green, it is well into the period of the year that is saturated with light. As early as the beginning of April, the days are significantly longer and lighter. By April, the birds have returned, and in May the seagulls and oyster catchers begin their hatching season on our stony shore, laying their fragile, remarkably camouflaged eggs in vulnerable nests amongst the stones by the fjord.

May is also a significant month for Norway, because one of the country's most important celebrations of national identity is "the 17th of May." And for Roman Catholics, May is traditionally the month of Mary. So it is rich for us here culturally, spiritually, and in nature. I shall begin by writing about Mary. There is a centuries-long tradition in the Church of celebrating

Our Lady in a special way by dedicating the month of May to her. It is fitting that a month so associated with the fertility and abundance of spring should be hers, since it was her fecundity of soul that brought forth Jesus into the world. Mary gave birth to *God*: in springtime, the earth throws off the harsh cold and darkness and bursts into new growth, green shoots rising from the soil. For me, May evokes images of blossoming cherry trees, soft candy-pink petals blown like fragrant confetti by the wind as spring progresses towards the fullness of summer. I think that for me the month of May is evocative of the beauty of Mary as the human being blessed with bearing God in her womb. The impact on each of us of her resounding YES to God is like the ripening of the human capacity for God, like a sweet blossoming after a long barrenness, like plump fruit appearing on a gnarled twig. Mary in her unparalleled fruitfulness is God-bearer, Theotokos.

In Cistercian life, we value an austere simplicity, so the Marian dedication of May does not consist of many external devotions. We have a beautiful white statue of Mary with the child Jesus in our cloister, and some of us pray briefly there every day, perhaps laying a hand on hers and the child's, or speaking to her in our hearts. This silent observance is characteristic of the Cistercian way and contains no less fervor for all its restraint. One sister here can often be seen in the early hours after Vigils, standing in silent contemplation before a painting of Mary and the infant Jesus, near her cell. These elements of our spiritual life are deeply personal, expressed in individual ways, but all in the Order are united by a profound love of Mary, to whom all our monasteries are dedicated. We are Tautra Mariakloster. Our Cistercian brothers an hour away are called Munkeby Mariakloster. Each of us takes the name of Mary as a part of our formal religious name at the time of Temporary Vows, even if that name is not used on a daily basis. While I am simply addressed as Sister Rafael, my full monastic name as a sister in First Profession is Maria Rafael.

Mary is loved for being the Mother of God, but she is also regarded as the perfect disciple, an intimate companion and a model for our lives. When I was in the Carmelite Order, I read about a holy man who described his religious life as "Mariform" life, and I internalized that phrase.

Every one of our Cistercian liturgical Offices throughout the day ends with an anthem to Mary. The Angelus, recalling the wonder of the incarnation, and celebrating Mary's "fiat," is rung three times a day, at Lauds, Sext, and the end of Compline. The *fiat*—"Be it done to me according to your word"—is a fundamental foundation of the surrender intrinsic to our monastic life. Such self-giving is intrinsic to all God-directed human life.

For me, the final line of the Angelus prayer gives impetus to my desire at the start of my day: "Pour forth, we beseech Thee, O Lord, thy grace into our hearts, that we, to whom the incarnation of Christ thy Son was made known by the message of an angel, may by his passion and cross be brought to the glory of his resurrection—through Christ, our Lord, Amen."

As I write this, in early March, it has just been announced that Pope Francis has declared a new Marian feast to be celebrated throughout the Roman Catholic Church from this year. It is the feast of Mary, Mother of the Church, and will be celebrated on the day after Pentecost. Another association with Blessed Mary in May!

Spring

What
at the sight of snowdrops
so rouses me; billows
like a sail in a sharp spring wind;
rides the swell
like a boat on its virgin voyage?

Light,
the springtime light.
It is *You*, jewel
shining from the ragged dark;
upon the shivering heart
refracting
perfect day.

Ah, now, the Tautra light: the spring is the start of the season of Norway's long illuminated days. Even by early April, the light can be sparkling and bright and seem on clear days of sunshine so like nearly-summer, it can be disorienting to realize that in fact the trees are still bare and there can still be random snowfalls. By May, the possibility of snow has receded and the light is spreading itself out beyond the boundaries of night. At 4:00, it is no longer deep darkness, but is like an infusion of soft light into the nearly-dark: a shadowy blue. We begin to wear our summer habits, as all the glass in our monastery heats up the house in the sunshine. When the days are warm in May, some of us start to swim in the fjord: a short dip before Vespers. The water is bracingly cold, some would say icy, but is wonderfully invigorating and is like a communion with the landscape.

The 17th of May is arguably the most important day in the Norwegian year—*Syttende mai*. This is Norwegian Constitution Day, which commemorates the definitive separation from Denmark and the establishment of the Norwegian Constitution in 1814. It wasn't until 1905, though, that Norway managed to separate entirely from Sweden. When I moved here, my knowledge of Scandinavian history was nil, and I was amazed to realize how recent the independence is. This fact explains the fervor of the distinctive and strong national feeling here, and also the passionate concern with language. A separate identity still needs nurturing. I am someone who has always been uncomfortable with a certain type of flag-waving patriotism. Perhaps in this I am of the generation accustomed to the ideal of the global village. So I was wary when I saw the way that on May 17 the Norwegians dress up in regional clothing and, yes, display flags galore. A number of homes on Tautra— including the monastery—have their own flagpole, and there are established "flag days" during the year. Here on our island, the celebrations take place in what is a village hall of sorts in the middle of the island. From outside, it is a plain, even austere white wood building, but on May 17, the interior is welcoming and cozy with long tables set out and a mouth-watering display of open-faced sandwiches (*smørbrød*) and large, light cream cakes with berries. A crowd of locals is all done up in the splendid regional dress, ready to chat, drink coffee, eat, sing, and watch an entertainment on the little stage by children (usually it seems to be a baton-twirling routine by children in white uniforms with brass band accompaniment). My critical reluctance was disarmed from the first time I experienced it. This is not an aggressive, triumphalist nationalism; it is something more wholesome, like fierce family pride. It is a celebration of a shared history and identity. The regional costumes, called *bunad*, are exquisite, with different colors and styles proclaiming one's area of origin. I admit to having secretly coveted many of the women's bunads that I've seen, with their feminine smock-like bodice and full, brightly patterned skirt.

Many of us from the monastery go to celebrate with our island neighbors after Mass every year. This past year it was covered by the local television network and took place at

Klostergården instead of the Tautra tun, the village hall. Klostergården is a well-known, attractive traditional inn at one end of the island, built beside the ruins of the original Tautra Cistercian monastery. This community was active from the 13th to the 16th centuries. Klostergården is renowned for its restaurant and its beers and juices (*saft*), made from its own berries. At the celebration last May, someone snapped a photograph of me clumsily trying my hand at baton-twirling. (How do the little ones do it so deftly?)

There is yet another highly significant date for us in May here on Tautra. Our monastic church was dedicated on May 12, 2007, an event that drew a large number of people to celebrate with the community, including Norway's Queen Sonja. This means that 2017 was a milestone anniversary for us: ten years since it was solemnly consecrated. I had never witnessed a church dedication until we attended the consecration of the new St. Olav's Cathedral in Trondheim last winter, and I was taken aback by the power of the rite. It seemed to me rather like a baptism, even though it is the dedication of a place. It is somehow deeply personal and historic, yet the promise of the ritual is accomplished over time. When a person is consecrated to the service of God, that is a graced event, an activity of the Holy Spirit, yet its potential is realized over the course of the person's life after the consecration. It is much the same with a church dedication. In the rite, it is striking with what dignity the altar is the focus. An extravagant abundance of oils is poured over the altar. Seeing this act, and then the priest wiping the oils from the broad stone surface, I found this locus of sacrifice and praise to become somehow remarkably personalized. The polished altar absorbs the spiritual blessing for us who pray the Mass around it, the Mass taking place on and around the altar, which is the living heart of the spiritual life flowing from a church consecration.

In the Trondheim cathedral dedication, I was able to appreciate the consecration of our own monastic church in a fresh way. Through this potent rite, the entire dedicated church is surrendered to its work of drawing people to the worship of God. This power to attract and to move transcends Mass attendance or even belief in God, when so many visitors enter the church here and find themselves aware of a sense of mysterious Presence by a rich and living silence. The dedication of the church is a hidden act underpinning this ministry of the place. Our daily liturgy—Mass, communal, and personal private prayer—stokes up the fire of a vibrant sacred presence who is always wherever people pray.

On the 12th of May, we celebrate a special liturgy in the monastery for this event in our monastic history, celebrating its present continuity. Small tealight candle holders, each surmounted by a wooden cross, are placed at intervals around the walls of the church and remain lit throughout the day of solemn festivity. The small crosses on the church walls are there permanently as a reminder of the dedication of the church. Like a baptism, on May 12, 2007, our monastic church was converted to a new life, growing gradually more fully into the life God intended for it. It became far more than a building, with an inner life more substantial by far than the architectural prizes it has won.

As the frozen ground of winter thaws, we begin to re-engage in garden work. We grow as many vegetables as we can in our modest plot of land, with the invaluable help of our volunteers, who work to prepare the ground as well as later to harvest its fruits. Our Irish chaplain, Fr. Anthony, has developed a remarkable shore-side kitchen garden using a seaweed-based soil. He can be seen doggedly wheeling barrows of seaweed from some distance along the shore, back to his garden near our boathouses, day after day, early in the season. By May, the hatching season on our stony shore has begun for seagulls and oystercatchers. The seagulls, defensively aggressive to human beings in their breeding season, are so accustomed to Anthony's presence working on his garden by the fjord that they usually ignore him. He produces spectacular lettuces of a large variety, which keep us in fresh salad from summer to October. He also grows parsley in abundance, beetroot, broccoli, radishes, and cabbage. Up nearer to the monastery, we grow carrots, green beans, peas, and squash. We all take delight in our berries: velvety fragrant raspberries, red currants that shine like gems on the bushes, aromatic black currants, and gooseberries, including sweet golden ones I'd never tasted before. There are colorful flowers, too, which we appreciate in Sister Hanne-Maria's arrangements for the church. We have a small, rather rickety greenhouse for growing tomatoes. I grew them for a couple of years with limited success, finding that many of them failed to ripen by the time the warmest weather disappeared at the end of the summer. Now Sr. Renata, a Junior Professed sister, has taken it on and done brilliantly. The seedlings are grown inside the house in early spring, then transplanted to spacious pots in the greenhouse. This past summer, many suppertimes were enhanced by a dish heaped with a crop of new tomatoes, and the homegrown tomatoes' taste is just delicious. They have a tangy, entirely distinctive sweet taste, utterly unlike shop-bought tomatoes. To me, the taste is like summer: a burst of green, of sunshine, of a sweet fertility.

By May, our guesthouses are usually busy. People often book far in advance to come and stay, coming from local areas and far-flung parts of Norway, Europe, and many other parts of the world. As Cistercians we live according the Rule of Saint Benedict, and hospitality is a central feature in Benedictine life. It is an expression of love. For us at Tautra Mariakloster, as a witness to Christian faith in a highly secular society and in a minority here as Roman Catholics, the guesthouses play an important part in the sharing of our life with others. People come as retreatants, with the explicit intention of being alone with God in an intense way for some days, or they come simply to rest, and to discover what is here in the quiet, in the landscape, in worship in our church, and in conversation with other guests and with sisters. Our guesthouses are old wooden buildings that were originally part of a farm, and the accommodation is comfortable and warm but simple. Some of the rooms have a view of the fjord, which is extraordinarily close to our monastery. The sight of the fjord provides a deep source of refreshment for visitors. Each guest is personally welcomed on arrival and shown to the guest room. There they find one of our soaps, distinctive to this monastery, on a folded towel on the bed. They find a horarium, but attendance at the Offices is not compulsory.

Most of our guests are not Catholic, and many are not affiliated to any church. But even those without any stated faith are drawn to come by some spiritual instinct. We have often seen in surprising ways how God's purposes have been carried out in the unexpected fruits of someone's stay here.

Volunteers are a vital part of our life too. They live in the guest accommodation and work with us for up to a year at a time. Most come for shorter periods of up to several months, and they clean the guesthouses, assist the cook in the kitchen, or work in the soap department, in the library, or in the garden. They are a terrific asset to us, and most volunteers say that they too benefit from the experience. Several of us in community were here first as volunteers, including me, although that outcome was never intended when the volunteer program was begun. Being here on a volunteer basis does allow a unique freedom to get a taste of the community's life from the margins, for anyone who is discerning his or her own vocation.

One feature of our day that some guests have deeply appreciated is our hour of silent adoration in the church after Vigils each morning, at 5:00. It is a time for simply being before God; in the dark season the silence offers a special anonymity that can make possible quiet tears or subtle gestures of prayer that one may feel too inhibited to expose in a well-lit church in company with others celebrating the liturgy. This time allows the discovery of encounter with God in solitude.

As enclosed contemplative nuns we have no active ministry, but the Solemnly Professed sisters are available to guests who feel the need or desire to talk with someone while they are staying here. This availability extends the witness provided by the monastery to a different level.

It strikes me very much, while writing about a particular month in our life, how rich each month, each day, actually is in this way of living, so ordinary on the surface, yet extraordinary in the depths. Each season has its distinctive gifts and challenges, but all are ultimately sources of joy and praise of our God, and of growth in his love.

Vulnerable as a Rock

Sr. Sheryl Frances Chen, OCSO

June is the brightest month, with the longest day of the year and its in-your-face beauty and abundance of life. June 21 has twenty hours and thirty-five minutes of daylight, and it never really gets dark before sunrise at 3:02. The trees have a full canopy of leaves, almost blocking our view of the fjord. They also make a living screen as tourist boats slow down and try to peer at the monastery through our live, leafy line at the shore.

The seagull couple that tried and failed to build a nest last year on the Zen rock outside our refectory returned this year and succeeded. During dinner most sisters were only half-listening to the reading, more fascinated by the seagulls gathering material for the nest and pressing it into proper nest-shape with their bodies. Three eggs appeared, and the parents dutifully sat on them through rain and sun and wind. Finally two chicks pecked their way out of their shells, and already on the second day they had been pushed out of the nest and had to learn to live on the ground, hiding in the tall grass from the sea eagle and magpies. Soon it was time for swimming classes and flight school, and we were delighted to see this year's brood grow up to be teenagers.

When the water temperature warms up to about 14 C (57 F!), Sr. Rafael and I go swimming in the fjord. We are careful not to step too close to the seagull nest that is near our boathouses. One day the nest was empty, and we were afraid the chicks had been eaten. Then we saw the two, waddling awkwardly down the middle of the path, right where we go to enter the water. We made our way intently toward the water's edge, looking carefully at the path and balancing rather precariously on the stones. When we reached the water's edge, we realized we no longer saw the chicks. Where had they gone? After floating a few minutes in the shockingly refreshing water, we waded ashore, dried off, and started walking back up the path. Suddenly we saw that one of the speckled rocks on the side of the path, only six inches from us, was actually a gull chick, hunkered down and immobile so as not to attract attention. We marveled at the perfect camouflage. Then we saw that one of the mottled rocks on the other side of the path was actually the other chick. As soon as we looked away from the first chick, we could no longer see it. It blended perfectly with the rocks on the shore.

June 29 is the Solemnity of Saints Peter and Paul, the foundation stones of the Church of Rome. Jesus says to Peter, "You are the rock." Did he mean that instead of sitting high on a throne, he should be like a seagull chick blending in with all the other rocks? As Pope Francis says, the shepherd should have the smell of the sheep: be the beautiful harmony of the rocks on the shore, each contributing to the whole, and supporting the others.

Sr. Rafael commented that the chick was actually quite vulnerable, its newly fluffed feathers making it seem larger than it really was. Only two days old, it cannot walk very fast, and it has not yet had flight or swimming lessons. It tumbles and stumbles over the stones to find a place of security. If the sea eagle flies over the exposed rocks at low tide, the chick has only its camouflage to protect it.

Maybe Jesus means that even a rock is vulnerable, and should be so. We are all rocks, living stones building up the church of Christ. Perhaps Jesus meant us to do so while accepting our vulnerability, and receiving help from the others whose speckled personalities and rough edges are oh-so-irritating. Are we not all fledglings under the shadow of Jesus' wings?

Jesus asks his disciples, "Who do people say that I am?" They answer, "Some say John the Baptist, others say Elijah or another of the prophets." Then he asks them, "Who do you say that I am?" Peter makes his confession of faith: "You are the Messiah!" Jesus asks us every day, Who do you say that I am? How do you experience me today?

A woman who has made a retreat at Tautra Mariakloster many times brought her Bible study group for a weekend retreat. She asked that I talk to them about our monastic life. One question took me by surprise: How did my relationship with Jesus change before and after I entered the monastery?

Before I entered I was intent on learning to be a Christian. I had professed Jesus as my Lord and Savior at seventeen and had been baptized in the Pacific Ocean. What did it mean to follow Jesus? I was falling in love with him, and I wanted to develop my prayer life. I came to see monastic life as the only way I could really give my life totally to him. So I entered the monastery thinking I was giving something to him, but also to get something for myself: a fruitful and lifegiving prayer life.

In the monastery, I discovered that our call is something much bigger than being faithful to praying in choir seven times a day. The total package of community life, trying to live the Gospel, is something much more demanding. I found that it is really Jesus who gives everything to me. Monastic life, says Br. Cyril, the old monk formerly at nearby Munkeby, is about learning to receive: to receive the gift of each moment, even if it doesn't seem as though it could be the Gospel or could possibly be God's will at the time. To learn to receive Jesus in my sister, and in every circumstance. I hope that as the puppy love feeling faded, my love for Jesus matured, as in a marriage. Instead of thinking about the Beloved all the time, I reach out with my love and attention to embrace a wider family.

We look out on the fjord from our cell windows and enjoy the panoramic view from our refectory and the altarpiece: the large plate glass windows behind the altar in church. The color of the water reflects the sky. On a sunny summer day, the fjord is blue, ranging from aquamarine to a deep navy. On a rainy day, the water's mood reflects the grayness of the clouds, sometimes looking almost black. We never get tired of watching the waves and the tides, always in flux. The weather changes every five minutes on Tautra. It is never boring.

The water in the fjord is a mixture, salt water on the bottom like the ocean and fresh water on top from melted snow and rainwater. It is international, the water from the fjord quickly merging into the North Atlantic current, bringing schools of young salmon with it. The salmon mature and feed in the open ocean and then return to spawn, amazingly finding the original river they came from. Some of the water must slip into the South Atlantic and then be swept into the South Indian and eventually the South Pacific current, swirling all the way to Hawaii. My mother was born on the Hawaiian island Lanai and grew up in Honolulu, and our family always had a love for the shore. Though I had spent many summers on the beach as a child, when I came to the island Tautra I realized that I had never lived so close to the water. I felt at home at the deepest place in me, in a way I never had any place else. I must have this affinity for water running in my blood, like a salmon seeking its original stream. Our cells are only about sixty meters from the waves gently lapping the line of seaweed at the high-tide mark. With the window open we can easily hear the waves breaking on the shoreline rocks.

Plankton grow in the brackish, conflicted layer of water between salt and fresh. Plankton is the beginning of the food chain: small fish feed on plankton, big fish eat the little fish, seals and dolphins and humans eat the big fish, and so on up the ladder to the largest carnivores. So all of life comes from this conflicted layer and from being mixed, like our community. We have very different personalities, very different backgrounds, and, because of our varied life experience, we have strong opinions—about the way things should be done in the monastery, about what to have for breakfast, about how to solve the world's problems, basically about everything.

The fact that conflict in the fjord is life-giving may be a paradigm for community life. Instead of shying away from conflicts with each other, we should rather welcome them as gifts of

God, a spark of life that bursts from rubbing and clinking against each other. If there are any novices who enter with romantic visions of how tranquil and quiet the monastery must be with the nuns praying in church seven times a day, they soon realize that our monastic community is just like any other human community: a mixed bag of personalities clashing against each other, even though we do have the common foundation of trying to live the Gospel.

When we have a hard time with someone else, it is tempting to avoid that person, and even to pray that God will call her somewhere else. If we can ask for and receive the grace of patience, and persevere through the situation or the relationship, often involving the demanding discipline of communication, we may discover the life that the conflict brings. We know that the red rocks on the shore were brought from Sweden by the glaciers that lay over Tautra for several centuries at the end of the last ice age. They have become beautifully rounded by hitting against one another and being tumbled in rough waters. After the storm, rocks of many different sizes, shapes, and colors nestle against one another, creating a wonderfully varied, international carpet that clothes and defines the island as it winds its way around the contours of Tautra.

There are two high tides and two low tides every twenty-four hours. We are amazed that all that water moves every six hours. I once actually witnessed the turn of the tide. It was my monthly hermit day, and I had walked to the southern point of the island, looking toward Trondheim fifteen kilometers (nine and a half miles) across the water while eating my knapsack lunch. I watched a particular rock at the water's edge as the waves gradually came higher and higher. Finally the rock was nearly submerged, and then the next wave was *lower*. Then the tide gradually receded, each wave coming not as high on the shore as the previous one. There was no fanfare, no neon sign blinking to signify the change. Just the quiet lapping of the waves as the water obeyed the tug of the gravity of the moon. Could conversion—a change of direction—actually be so easy? Back and forth, up and down, bit by bit, every six hours. Just obey the tug of Jesus on the heart.

The difference between high and low tide here is quite large—about 1.8 meters. The land drops rather steeply off at the place where we go swimming. It can be scary to take three steps, then suddenly drop off a ledge and be in water over our heads. Water can be calming, but it can also be frightening. I think of the Japanese martyrs discussed in Shusako Endo's *Silence* who were crucified on the beach at low tide. Their executioners had only to wait six hours and let the rising tide slowly and inexorably drown their victims.

Life is tough at the shore. Living on the island of Tautra with its nesting seagulls and oyster catchers, we experience the screeching and excitement of the seabirds whenever the sea eagle comes soaring over the beach looking for breakfast. We cheer for the frantic parents and hope that the eggs and chicks survive the morning smorgasbord selection unscathed. We are reminded that life is fragile and vulnerable; it's dangerous out there in the lullifyingly beautiful scenery on the shore. But Thomas Merton takes the part of the predator as an image of contemplative prayer.

> Suddenly I became aware of great excitement. The pasture was full of birds—starlings. There was an eagle flying over the woods. The crows were all frightened, and were soaring, very high, keeping out of the way. Even more distant still were the buzzards, flying and circling, observing everything from a distance. And the starlings filled every large and small tree, and shone in the light and sang. The eagle attacked a tree full of starlings but before he was near them the whole cloud of them left the tree and avoided him and he came nowhere near them. Then he went away and they all alighted on the ground. They were there moving about and singing for about five minutes. Then, like lightning, it happened. I saw a scare go into the cloud of birds, and they opened their wings and began to rise off the ground and, in that split second, from

behind the house and from over my roof a hawk came down like a bullet, and shot straight into the middle of the starlings just as they were getting off the ground. They rose into the air and there was a slight scuffle on the ground as the hawk got his talons into the one bird he had nailed.

It was a terrible and yet beautiful thing, that lightning flight, straight as an arrow, that killed the slowest starling.[1]

Merton is inspired by the hawk because, he says, "it knows its business," and a monk's business is prayer. If only our every thought of God or love flew like a dart to pierce the heart of Jesus!

As my confessor said to me when I was in temporary vows, "Unless you intend to go to the top of the mountain, don't even waste your time messing around at its base." Our aim should be straight, and our intention is necessarily intense.

Yet there is only so much *we* can do. If we are faithful to our call and to being formed to the life being lived in a particular community, we discover that God is asking much more of us—as Merton describes his routine—than training our bodies to get up in the middle of the night (in Merton's day it was 2:00 a.m.), fasting more than half the year, doing heavy farmwork while wearing cumbersome woolen habits, and spending hours in a cold church singing psalms in an incomprehensible language[2] and prostrating on the floor for mistakes made in either the chant or the many prescribed ceremonies. All for Jesus, with a smile! as Dom James Fox famously repeated.

God's call opens out, and opens us. God demands that we grow beyond ourselves and begin to see that our vocation is not just for the salvation of our own souls, but connects us

---

[1] February 10, 1950. *The Sign of Jonas* (New York: Doubleday, 1956), 267–68.
[2] It was six years before some of us immigrants could begin to understand hymns in Nynorsk.

with every human being on the planet. Merton had his
Damascus experience at Fourth and Walnut in Louisville. For
others it is a slowly dawning insight that one is faced with
many small choices each day: to choose one's own preferences,
or to "put on the things of the monastery" and learn to hold
all things in common, even ideas and what one does with one's
body.[3] For Merton, this meant maintaining a wide correspondence with a broad range of people, as seven published volumes of letters attest. How could he have had time for this
tremendous output (even though he could dictate to three
secretaries simultaneously) while living the minutiae of Trap-
pist life? It could only be because he could channel his intel-
lectual gifts and focus his energy on the single goal of attaining
the summit of his seventh mountain.

As Merton prepared for solemn vows, he wrote of the all-
encompassing love of God that lies behind everything the
monk does and is the goal of monastic life:

> God's love takes care of everything I do. He guides me
> in my work and in my reading. . . . God has put me in
> a place where I can spend hour after hour, each day, in
> occupations that are always on the borderline of prayer.
> There is always a chance to step over the line and enter
> into simple and contemplative union with God. . . .
> I have got in the habit of walking up and down under the
> trees or along the wall of the cemetery in the presence of
> God. . . . I did not come here for myself but for God.
> God is my order and my cell. He is my religious life and
> my rule. He has disposed everything in my life in order
> to draw me inward, where I can see Him and rest in Him.
> He has put me in this place because He wants me in this

---

[3] RB 58.26, The Procedure for Receiving Brothers: "Then and there in the
oratory, he is to be stripped of everything of his own that he is wearing and
clothed in what belongs to the monastery" (RB 1980, ed. Timothy Fry [College-
ville, MN: Liturgical Press, 1981], 270–71).

place, and if He ever wants to put me anywhere else, He will do so in a way that will leave no doubt as to who is doing it.[4]

Monastic life, said Br. Cyril of Munkeby, is about learning to receive. All that happens to us, not only the restful and sweet moments of contemplation, but also the irritating brother or sister, the haughty superior, and even real injustices and sins against us, are a message from God to bring us closer to himself. It is a terrible thing to fall into the hands of the living God. He will consume you. The monk does not just fall into his hands. He runs headlong into that consuming embrace. A Cistercian is formed in the fourth degree of humility, when a monk embraces difficult, contrary, and unjust things with a quiet heart. Patience is the name of the game. Sometimes all you can do is embrace the ache, the empty space, the seeming absence of the Lover. This hollows us out and makes us capable of receiving more and embracing more, in imitation of the kenosis (self-emptying) of Christ. We make one vow, said my novice mistress: to go all the way.

The great solemnity of Pentecost often falls in June. Dom Christian de Chergé, the prior of our monastery of Atlas, who was martyred along with six of his brothers and portrayed in the film *Of Gods and Men*, said of this feast,

> The great creator of this revolution is the Spirit whose proper joy is to have nothing of its own, to be nothing but gift, totally dependent on the one who receives it: Like fire that waits for something combustible in us; like water that looks for a channel in us in which to circulate. The poor know this: because they have nothing, they are available to the grace that comes.[5]

---

[4] January 14, 1947. Merton, *Sign of Jonas*, 30.
[5] Christian de Chergé, *L'invincible espérance* (Paris: Bayard Èditions, 1997), 263 (my translation).

Like water. Water surrounds us and is constantly before our eyes. It naturally seeks the lowest place. It finds the smallest opening to flow through. It washes over the rocks at the shore and filters down into the narrow, dark, sometimes clogged minuscule canyons in between. It picks up and bears away debris and garbage at every high tide. It patiently wears down the sharp edges and fissure lines of each individual stone so that after eons, they fit snuggly together and become a safe foundation for nesting birds. A few more eons, and they are on their way to becoming sand. In God's time, that's just the blink of an eye—an *øyeblikk* in Norwegian.

Merton spoke prophetically of the love of God as a fire. It is not lost on readers of *The Seven Storey Mountain* who know the circumstances of his death that he himself was burned as he sought the Christ of the burnt men. The fact that he died in Bangkok of accidental electrocution while participating in interreligious monastic dialogue shows that his perspective had been broadened. The monk is *monos*—often geographically alone, but also integrated in himself with the one goal of seeking God. In dialogue with Buddhists we discover the One Reality common to all seekers. While preparing for ordination, Merton wrote,

> The fire of love for the souls of men loved by God con-
> sumes you like the fire of God's love, and it is the same
> love. It burns you up with a hunger for the supernatural
> happiness, first of people that you know, then of people
> you have barely heard of and finally of everybody . . .
> this hunger is exactly the same as the hunger for your
> own personal union with God, but now it includes some-
> one else.[6]

The great Easter-Ascension-Pentecost cycle is the season for the sacrament of confirmation, in both the Roman Catholic and the Lutheran churches. Norway nears the millennium celebra-

[6] October 15, 1948. Merton, *Sign of Jonas*, 132.

tion of its Christianization by Saint Olav, who died in the battle
of Stiklestad in 1030. We sisters who come from the United
States notice a weird hybrid of cultures in Norwegian society.
While in some ways it is even more secularized than the US,
it has been a Christian country for so long that some of the
church holidays and traditions have become part of the secular
calendar. Christmas and the day after, Easter and the day after,
and Pentecost and the day after are all national holidays. The
whole country shuts down from midday on Holy Thursday
until the third day after Easter. Many people celebrate the vigil
of Saint John the Baptist, June 23, with bonfires on the beach.
An ordinary newspaper might report that "this new hotel will
open in time for Pentecost," while in the US, people generally
have no idea when Pentecost is or what it celebrates. Secular
society has even borrowed Catholic terms: school children can
choose between having church confirmation or civil confirmation. The latter is a coming-of-age ceremony, marking a ninth-
grader's place and responsibility as an adult in secular
society.

June is the month when we celebrate more solemnities than
in any other. Pentecost ushers in the great feasts of Ordinary
Time: Trinity Sunday, Body and Blood of Christ (formerly
called Corpus Christi), Sacred Heart, and the solemnities that
commemorate the birth of John the Baptist and the founding
saints of the church of Rome. It is as if the outpouring of the
spirit at Pentecost multiplies the graces received, so the church
cannot stop celebrating the central mystery of our faith, the
bodily resurrection of Jesus from the dead, even as we leave
the paschal season and re-enter ordinary time. In the monastery, no time is ordinary; all time is extraordinary, bathed in
the light and mercy of God, if we are aware enough to receive
it. On solemnities we have the day free, except for two sisters
to cook the dinner and two sisters to take portress duty (answering the phone and doorbell). We celebrate a more festive
Mass, usually with extra music on the organ or harp, and we
have a "better midday meal" than on ferial days. The holiday

is an opportunity for those sisters who wish to take a long walk in the forest (yes, we have some forest on Tautra!) or walk the two kilometers to the Cistercian ruins and the lighthouse, risking dive-bombing and screeching gulls.

Because I was a convert to Catholicism, the solemnity of the Sacred Heart is one that had to grow on me. I guess I had seen too much kitsch art that looked as though Jesus was holding a bleeding tomato, and that did not inspire my devotion. I don't think I even knew what I was looking at. While I was at Mississippi Abbey, I was given a photo of a modern painting of the Good Shepherd. At first glance it seemed to be only that: the Good Shepherd with a presumably lost-and-found lamb slung across his shoulders. A closer look, however, revealed the lamb licking the nail wound in Jesus' hand, even sticking its tongue into it.

The lamb licks the wound, cleansing and soothing it. The shepherd who will bind up the wounded is himself wounded. By licking the blood, the lamb also "drinks from the wellsprings of salvation." As the letter to the Romans says, this is the blood that justifies us, that saves us from the wrath of God, that is, Judgment. Even in his resurrected body, Jesus bears the wounds of his passion. The wound is still open. I can imagine that the shepherd even offered his wound to the lamb, as he did to Thomas. Here! Touch me, taste me. "All you who are thirsty, come and drink!"

What we have most in common with each other, and with those who visit us, is our woundedness, our human condition. We can deepen our bonds with one another if we have the courage to be vulnerable with one another. In some mysterious way, I believe our wounds can nourish another person. Apparently blood still issues from the Good Shepherd's hand, and it nourishes the lamb who receives Jesus' lifeblood. As I think back over a wound I received in the past, whether justly or unjustly, I wonder what I have learned from it that can be said to issue forth from the wound, that is lifegiving to others? Perhaps it is the sister who causes me some trouble, costs me an outpouring of energy and a change in my plans for the day, on whom I can rest in some mysterious way, if I accept in faith that God's Providence has sent me this trouble.

The shepherd, when he finds the lost sheep, calls his friends and neighbors to rejoice with him. It is a communal celebration. Some would say that we can have a party as long as there's cake, but it's much more fun if we can share it with a crowd who will enjoy it. Jesus invites us as community to share his joy when each of us has a turn to ride on his shoulders and to give rest to his head. Each of us has a chance to drink from his wounds and, if we dare, to allow each other to see our vulnerable places, whether of body or behavior—even to allow another gently to probe the place of injury. Somehow, offering our wounds to another is lifegiving for the other as well as healing for ourselves. There is something about seeing another's vulnerability that enables us to love more and gives us the courage to be ourselves more vulnerable. This sharing at a deeper, scarier level binds us more closely as community.

There has been much discussion in our Cistercian Order recently about what leadership looks like today. At a recent mixed general meeting, Abbot Peter McCarthy made an intervention that I think is very beautiful. He said that when he first became abbot, his image of his task was the Good Shepherd, the one who pretty much has his act together and can help others. After some years of experience, he said the image changed to the man with the withered hand whom Jesus healed on the Sabbath. Jesus asks him to come forward and stretch out his hand in the midst of the crowd so he can heal it. A shepherd is one who is wounded, knows it, and has the courage to show his weakness in the midst of the community.

Michael Casey says,

> Contemplation is the fruit of radical self-honesty and of kindness to others. As we look upon the Father with the eyes of Christ we are rapt in contemplation. As we look on people through the same eyes, we find that we are

drawn into compassion. Contemplation and compassion are inseparable. Love is indivisible. The love poured into our hearts by the Spirit not only joins us to God; it also increases our solidarity with those around us through recognizing their lovableness and bearing their burdens with equanimity and even a measure of joy.[7]

As the twelfth-century Cistercian abbot Guerric of Igny wrote in his fourth sermon for Palm Sunday, Jesus' side was opened that we might have a way into his heart.[8] Our heart becomes Jesus' heart and becomes expanded by that love that bears all things. Tolerating each other's weaknesses becomes easier, and even a joy, because then we are like Christ, whose heart was fully human, pierced both by our sins and our love. Beatrice of Nazareth, a thirteenth-century Cistercian nun, says that those who enter into the heart of Jesus find the freedom to be fully themselves: "She is like a fish that swims in the breadth of the ocean and rests in the depths. She is like a bird that flies in the spaciousness and height of the sky. Thus she experiences her spirit as walking unbound in the depth and spaciousness and height of love."[9]

Beatrice would have been at home on Tautra with its 800-meter-deep fjord, many birds, and wide-open sky. All these aspects of nature are a daily reminder to us of the depth and spaciousness and height of God's love. May we, on a bright June day, and every day of the year, enter Jesus' broken body through one of his many wounds and rest there, close to his

[7] Michael Casey, *Fully Human, Fully Divine: An Interactive Christology* (Liguori, MO: Liguori/Triumph, 2004), 207.

[8] "Blessed is he who, in order that I might be able to build a nest in the clefts of the rock, allowed his hands, feet and side to be pierced and opened himself to me wholly" (Guerric of Igny, *Liturgical Sermons*, vol. 2, trans. the Monks of Mount Saint Bernard Abbey, CF 32 (Kalamazoo, MI: Cistercian Publications, 1971), 77.

[9] *Vita Beatricis* 3.14.258: The Sixth Degree of Love, in *The Life of Beatrice of Nazareth, 1200–1268*, trans. and annot. Roger De Ganck, with John Baptist Hasbrouck, CF 50 (Kalamazoo, MI: Cistercian Publications, 1991), 317.

heart. May we enter more deeply into the body that is our own community if we dare, through the wounds of another, to find at the center our heart, which is Jesus' own.

Memories of Summer Silence

Sr. Hanne-Maria Berentzen, OCSO

Silence. The whole world around me is silent. The first day of July, and the summer has finally come. June was cold and windy; only the light during the night said *summer*. It was a blessing, though, since May gave us two very warm weeks, and nature didn't know what to do about it. A cool June gave some balance, but hardly any rain. Where do we go with the climate changes?

As I walk through the pasture and woods, I notice the lack of wild flowers. Where the spruce gives shadow, there is green grass, but in open land it is yellow and brown, like what I used to see when traveling in Europe. We are blessed with fresh green nature so far north, and we are grateful to avoid the heat.

Now the summer is very welcome. We need it to live through another winter. Feeling the welcoming heat of the sun, enjoying the cooling breeze. No breeze today, only quiet and calm. Not even the aspen leaves move. A warbler is singing, joined by a blackbird.

Suddenly there is a sweet fragrance filling the air: What is it? I see no rose bushes here. The scent is very strong. As I move on, I discover a white clover field between the nettles. "This is what I cannot explain for my friends in Germany," my niece used to say, "what it means that it *smells* Norway." Maybe it is the wild flowers, this beauty God has thrown out everywhere in summer.

Two bluebells have come out in the green of the shadow. "The bluebell week" ("Blåklokkevikua") sings in my heart, a song about summer this particular week when the bluebells start blossoming. It is always in time for the feast of Saint

Thomas, July 3rd. Bluebells are flowers of perseverance. They are so tender, yet they seem to survive any weather, asking very little of the soil. They grow high in the mountains and blossom till the frost comes. Together with yarrow and red clover I can pick them for the bouquet by the icon of Our Lady until Mid-November.

Saint Thomas in the midst of bluebells—the one whose doubt was so important for the church that it had to be proclaimed as part of the Gospel. He was brave, saying "Come, let us go to die with him" (John 11:16). When they arrested Jesus a few days later, he fled with the others. Why was he not with them behind locked doors that first Easter night when the others tried to grasp the reality of the resurrection?

I find Thomas encouraging. His stubborn doubt opens my own doubts: What are my doubts? How do I not believe the consequences of the resurrection? Thomas, help me face my lack of faith, and I can start anew, growing in trust.

Summer. July is summer, regardless of temperature. No darkness through the night. Over and over it sings in me, "Darkness is not dark for you; the night is bright as the day" (Ps 139:12). That is here, in the stars of winter and the white clouds on light sky in summer. The sun is shining when I go to bed, and the sun is up when we rise for Vigils. We cannot beat the sun, just as we cannot look her in the eye when she hardly gets up in Midwinter.

The weather and climate are important means to turn us to God. Although we have a great responsibility to change our life style and care for the climate, in daily life it is out of our control; the weather is what it is, and we have to adjust, receive and adjust.

I still need to put on a windbreaker when I go for a bike ride in the early morning. As soon as I leave our property, it smells of the feast of Saints Peter and Paul, June 29. Every year the neighbor is spreading the manure just in time for the Solemnity of these great apostles, and the smell will last for several days. It must have been the same in Clairvaux at the time of Saint

Bernard: in his second sermon for this feast, he talks about the manure in our spiritual life. I like to read his sermons every year when the day comes. Saint Bernard is so rooted in nature in his spirituality. The manure smells bad, but is necessary for fertility. If we want to bring fruit in our life, we have to accept the bad smell of our rotting waste. What a blessing to live in an environment where there are still livestock. We can still smell the manure in the spring and after the haying, when there is another spreading to promote the second cutting in August.

Routine opens my senses and my mind to a deeper awareness of reality. This year I have squeezed a bike ride into the morning schedule, over the causeway to the bridge. Our enclosure ends at the bridge, well marked by a public gate. When Queen Sonja opened the new bridge and laid the cornerstone for our new monastery, she said that the bridge was built for the benefit of snails and nuns. The bridge opened the water and currents in a way necessary for the growth of sea snails, important food for the birds of our nature sanctuary.

Biking moves the whole body, almost like skiing and swimming. I discover that my mind and body are better fit to meet the challenges of the day after this morning ride. It opens me up for better focusing in prayer, as well as a deeper joy and gratitude. Doing the same every morning frees my energy and increases my awareness:

Seven curlews fly up in front of me. Is it two families or one? The chicks are already so big that it is hard to judge who is grown and who is not. Could it be five chicks? Or two young ones from last year learning how to be parents? As I leave the island, biking on the two-kilometer causeway into the fjord, I look for the Shel duck. A mother and a half-grown chick are feeding in the seaweed on the northern side of the road. It must be our most beautiful duck, with black, brown, and green colors on the white body. One morning I counted two of the ducks with eleven chicks. Since then I have seen no more than one chick with the two grown ones. Is it the same family, or does this one live further out and just happen to be here this day? Or have predators eaten the ten chicks?

The eider swimming further out still has her five chicks and two daughters from last year to help her. Thank God! The sea gulls are sitting peacefully along the causeway. They are used to traffic and do not cry out as much as those on our shore.

God protect our young ones from all kind of predators!

Living on the island has changed my views on many things. Now I see the beauty in the large parts of sand covered with seaweed at low tide. I used to find the seaweed ugly. Now I see the beauty of the different kinds of seaweed, and I notice where it is in its growth. The colors change all through the year, from yellow to bronze and red/brown to black. During the summer it shows how low the tide is, and it makes us aware of the full moon. When we have no darkness, it is easy to forget about the moon and how important the phase of the moon is for all of nature. At low tide you can walk for hours on the bottom of the fjord before the tide comes in again: crossing the Red Sea.

I am surprised by the sudden sound of strong waves, beating in on the shore. No ship out there, no wind. It lasts for about fifteen minutes, as if the water is shifting mood. Then it goes back to normal. It is the tide coming in. The currents can be very strong. I have to check how they move before swimming from the shore. When they are strong, we must carefully discern how and where to swim so that we can come back. Sometimes you swim and swim and get nowhere. The difference between high and low tide is about 1.8 meters (six feet). Watching and experiencing this energy in the mass of the water makes me humble.

In July the fjord is slowly warming up. Our Viking sisters have started to take their daily swim in the late afternoons. I am content to dip in and get quickly up. The cold water is refreshing. One sunny day I find it warm enough to swim. The chicks of the sea gulls are already in the water, their parents diving angrily towards my head. Tiny me in the huge fjord, on the same level as the beeping chicks. It changes my outlook

on life. Being carried by the waves and the water is a strong
experience of God. It takes trust to relax and float, but then the
waves can come, and I let myself be moved with the waves.

The composition of the community has changed. This becomes evident on July 4. With nine different nationalities in
the community, we no longer celebrate the American day of
the Constitution with a picnic. I raise the flag on the pole before
Mass in honor of our Queen Sonja. It is her birthday. The blue
and white cross on the red flag proclaims festivity in the neigh-
borhood. It is a joy to remember the queen and the royal family
in our prayers. She has been very good to us. In 2003 she came
to lay the cornerstone for our monastic church, and we had
the privilege of hosting her overnight. She came back for the
celebration of the Dedication of the Church four years later.
Raising the flag for the queen and praying for America during
Mass bring happy thoughts.

America has given us so much, the foundation of our monastery, six of our sisters, the continued support from our
motherhouse Our Lady of the Mississippi Abbey, our grandmother house in Wrentham, and the many other American
monasteries of our Order. Our good friends in the US continue
to pray for us, visit us, and support us. Although three of our
American sisters have now become Norwegian citizens, our
gratitude for what the US has given us is deep and lasting.

In 2006 we had planned to celebrate July 4 in the new monastery. God had a better plan. When the officials came from
the town on Monday July 3 to authorize the construction of
the building so we could move in, they said no. The construc-
tors had to work another week before we could take it over.
How inconvenient!

Father Joël of Cîteaux, the mother house of our Order, was
coming on the 7th to stay for half a year of sabbatical with us.
He would stay in the old house once we moved out. Now we
had to send him to the bed-and-breakfast inn on the island.
Our prioress, Sr. Rosemary, had strictly forbidden us to tell
anybody when we were moving in: "I do not have the capacity

to serve any coffee that day," she said. We kept our mouths shut. Then one of the leaders of our Capital Campaign in the US asked if his daughter and son-in-law could come at that time, and of course we said yes. They slept in the parlor. The pastor in Trondheim called: I really need a break: Please can I come for a few days? I will bring a sleeping bag and stay with Fr. Anthony. "I cannot say no to Father Dominic," said Sr. Rosemary. "And," continued Fr. Dominic: "Remember the student I told you about? I think she has a vocation. Can I bring her with me?" The only place we had for her was a room in the boathouse.

In the afternoon of July 10th we took ownership of the new monastery. Our first prayer in the new church was the first Vespers of Saint Benedict: when we celebrated our first Mass in the new church, it was July 11, the solemnity of this monastic father, and Cîteaux was present, concelebrating at the altar.

Cîteaux in Norway, for the first time in history, as far as we know. The monks of our Order lived here in three monasteries for three centuries during the medieval period, and probably also nuns of our order in Nonneseter in Bergen. The abbots traveled to Cîteaux for the general chapter, but we don't know that anybody from Cîteaux would go so far North. It was God's plan, not ours, that Fr. Joël should be here for the first Mass in our new church. Looking back, it was the seed of what is now Munkeby Mariakloster, a small community of monks from Cîteaux.

We were not alone that day. The vicar general came since the bishop was not in town. He stopped overnight with our sisters of the Bonifatius Secular Institute in Levanger. The four of them came, dressed up for the solemnity and special day. They are our forerunners in Benedictine life in Norway; they started their mission in our county in 1964. What was more fitting than celebrating this day with them? Here we were, eight sisters and our chaplain, Cîteaux, the diocese, our sisters representing our parish, Fr. Dominic, the student from Saint Olav's parish in Trondheim, and the young American couple with the baby in the mother's womb. They were Episcopalian and Presbyterian, and they brought the ecumenical aspect that is so important in our life here. A week earlier we would have been alone. We served coffee after Mass.

The Feast of Saint Benedict carries this beautiful message for me: we may be tired, we may want more space, more solitude, more silence. Yet hospitality is a basic Benedictine and Christian feature. In our search for God he will remind us again and again that our life is a life given. The claims of hospitality will pull us out of our own comfort zone. If we can follow Christ also then, he will give us the strength we need. This is not easy learning for me. Yet the years at Tautra have made me realize how important it is, not just for our guests, but for us. The guests are as important for us as we are for them.

"Guests are never lacking in the monastery," says Saint Benedict.

The memories of the past are formative elements of the celebration. On this feast it expands my deep gratitude for our monastery, this monastic church, this community. This particular year it is also a day of special gratitude for the growth of the community. Sr. Agnes is making her first vows. I was sure I would finish the two scapulars for her a week beforehand. My plans and wishes and efforts were thrown up in the air and scattered. An unexpected meeting takes a whole afternoon. Translation work is asked for with short deadline. A sister has a doctor's appointment, and I must help in the soap department.

Trust, trust, trust. Finding the balance between wise and prudent organization, openness to others' needs and not neglecting my own and my own responsibilities. Trusting and caring and listening to when to say Yes and when to say No. Discernment is a matter of the moment, not just of big decisions.

I finish both scapulars in due time, and make the breakfast pastry. The bouquet of roses is ready for the altar. "Oh, Blessed Father, Benedict."

Sr. Agnes has come shining out of her retreat, ready for the big day. Sr. Anne Elizabeth is playing the organ for First Vespers. The celebration has begun. Our new sub-chantresses are well prepared to sing the antiphons.

"What do you seek?" asks our prioress. A few days later the reading about the prophet Elijah at Mount Tabor confronts us: How long will you limp to both sides?

What do I seek? Now, today. Oh Lord, help me always to seek you and nothing else. Not me, not my preferences, not what I think is best, but only you and what you see as best. This gives the freedom even to make the wrong decisions, and bad decisions. A great freedom and great responsibility. It takes time to see, to quiet down, and to know my emotions that can so easily fool me.

In her talk to Sr. Agnes this morning Sr. Brigitte points out the realism of Saint Benedict. In his wisdom he makes clear for the beginner that the way of life is not easy. Since monks are always beginners even after fifty years of monastic life, we should be well prepared for the difficulties that meet us on our life's journey. This realism opens for a deep joy. The smell of the manure for the feast of Saints Peter and Paul, the joy of knowing what comes before the sweet scent of honey in the clover meadow and the wild roses.

July is the peak of the summer, yet already the beginning of the harvest. Every day Fr. Anthony brings in a bucket full from the vegetable garden. Lettuce in green and purple, radishes and parsley. Now come the small roots from the thinning of beets, parsnips, and celery. We use it all. The sisters have a smaller vegetable garden, adjusted to the time we can spend there.

"Are you pulling them out?" asks a volunteer when I show her how to thin the vegetables. It is her first experience of preparing the soil, fertilizing, weeding, sowing, and thinning. If you skip anything in the process, you may not get a harvest, or only a very poor harvest. This is the realism of monastic discipline and Cistercian simplicity. The more we fall back into the weeds of our society, the more scattered our mind becomes, and the less fruit we will produce. Cultivating your own food increases gratitude. You know life is not a grocery store.

One day our neighbor Kjersti gives us a crate of four hundred kilos of potatoes. Now we need all the space we have for cooling. Living next to a potato field has many advantages! One year another neighbor came into the kitchen saying, "I brought you some carrots." When we came out, there was a crate of six hundred kilos. Some went into buckets of sand for the winter, as many as we could process were frozen, and we discovered that you can freeze them raw when thinly sliced and use them as salad in the winter. God's generosity never stops surprising us and teaching us new ways to receive.

July is vacation time. Our guesthouses are full, and we are making dinner for close to thirty people a day. Serving naturally grown vegetables and fruits of our own or our neighbors' produce is a special gift we can give them. "Untraveled food," as the farmers say. More important is the sharing of our liturgy, rhythm, and silence with others.

"Good to have you with us again," I say to a guest. "It is so good to be here. And you know, now I can enter more easily into the silence." A former volunteer is coming back for a week of her vacation. It has been four years since I saw her. I comment on how well she looks. She looks like a different person from when she first came and asked to talk with me. "I am so grateful for the flexibility you sisters gave me when I was here. That helped me so much. I needed these years to find my physical, mental, and spiritual strength again."

Thank God that we can be a place that gives people more space and time than the pressure they meet in the society, a place where a few people can enter a silence that opens them to the experience of the love and mercy of God.

July is the prime time for roses. The first ones start in June: small white and pink wild roses strewn over high green bushes with sharp thorns. Tautra has a great variety of wild rosehip roses, and they blossom well into the first weeks of July. Together with the Norwegian thyme they mark the nature of the island. The scent of the thyme blends with the tiny field strawberries in a Paradise experience. On the fjord side behind the church is the cemetery with a hedge of bright red roses. As soon as July starts, you see the spots of the red buds, and within a week the whole hedge is joyfully red and green. When the loosestrife also start blooming with their plentiful yellow spears, my mind starts preparing for *Olsok*, the feast of our national saint, King Olav Haraldson (995–1030) on July 29. Some years the roses and loosestrife are late, but they are always there for *Olsok*, when we need the red and the yellow to mirror the old royal colors of the national weapon and the martyr's glory. God provides what we need at the right time. Some of the roses may blossom until Advent begins, so we can use our own flowers for the altar.

I am going to our brothers at Munkeby Mariakloster for a few days to focus on writing these chapters. The last months at home have been too busy. I start out as a pilgrim, hoping the best for the weather, although we are praying for rain. I try to make my backpack light.

The brothers cannot pick me up at the railway station, and I decide to walk the four miles to the monastery. A maxi taxi picks me up at home for the price of a bus ride in the city, a privileged service in our rural town. We are picking up other passengers at different places. We are driving up a tiny road by a farm, winding into the woods, and ending at a house by a lake, very secluded and beautiful. A grandmother is taking her visiting ten-year-old granddaughter to the city for a shopping day. The world is full of perfect places for hermit life. As we discover them, they become places of solitude inside us. The commuter train has a silent wagon, and the view of the landscape is nice.

"Take the road over the bridge," was Brother Bruno's advice. Levanger is a small city. I was immediately out of downtown and city busyness, walking through an old residential area. Being a city girl of origin, I enjoy these short visits to the city, walking the streets for some minutes praying for the people who have their daily life here—all these very ordinary places with very ordinary people, each of whom is a mystery. Every house has something of Paradise in it. I notice the neat gardens, flowers, bushes, and lawns that speak of joy and standards of good lives.

July is the time for pilgrims going to the shrine of Saint Olav. We have already had four of them at Tautra. Now I join them with my little walk.

Farms, pasture, and cattle replace the residences. The morning hours are gone, the sun is hot. Seldom if ever have I experienced such heat in our region. I decide on a water break every half hour. A small cup of water and two-minute stop gives new energy. This morning we had the gospel about giving somebody a cup of water for the sake of Christ. Only when you really thirst do you understand what this means. As I stop, I turn around and receive a soft light breeze. The view of the town, the farms, woodlands, fields, and blue fjord is beautiful. Distant mountains are rising in different shadows in the north. At Tautra we see the distant mountains south and east and west; here they see them in the north, seemingly with wider areas of wilderness.

Is it worth taking an hour extra on the journey by walking, saving money for a taxi? I decide it is. We easily get a commercial attitude towards time and miss important aspects of life. Walking with a backpack and a stick prepares me well for the job ahead. I walk the gospel of this Sunday: Jesus called the twelve to himself and sent them out two by two. He told them not to bring all the extras I have in my back pack, not even a staff, which I find so helpful. He let them wear sandals. I made sandals my choice. It turned out to be a good one. No blisters. I repeat the gospel to myself as I walk.

It is less dry here. The fields are like slow waves in different greens through the landscape. At home the barley fields are already turning yellow and soft. Here they are still green and have not yet lowered their heads. Still young and proud, without the moving softness of riper time. The barley fields are my favorites, always moving as they grow more and more fertile.

The carrots have grown higher here; they had more snow and a later spring, and this is good for the crop. Now they have heat and all the light through the night that makes everything grow high.

I am keeping up with the time and hope to arrive for Sext. Behind the fields the wooded hills are rising. That is where I am going. First down to cross the river just before it pours out in a waterfall. I have often come here by car, but never seen or heard the waterfalls. Walking takes me into the landscape in a different way. I look to see if there is a path following the river, so I could walk by the ruins of the medieval monastery of Munkeby, but no, I'd better stay on the road.

I arrive in time for Sext. The tiny chapel of the brothers is so different from our big church. This is a monastery in the woods; our five brothers are singing the Office softly in the small room surrounded by birch trees. I enjoy the complementary differences between our two communities. It is nice to be with our brothers a few days.

I am back home for the new Feast of Saint Mary Magdalene on July 22. Less than three weeks after the feast of Saint Thomas we focus again on the resurrection. I guess we women have a special affinity to this feast, in gratitude that Jesus chose first to appear to a woman after the resurrection, and that she was the first to hear "Go and tell!" We have a special commemoration praying Tierce in the memorial garden of July 22, 2011, when seventy-seven people were killed by a man in and near Oslo, with many others wounded. The bombing of the government building and the Utøya shooting of children and teenagers shocked our nation and the world, and we decided to make a memorial garden next to our church. Every day we strike a gong there for the Angelus after Sext, in commemoration of the dead and all those wounded in terrorist actions.

Can we ever fathom the reality of the resurrection of Christ? Pope Benedict XVI emphasizes so beautifully the paradigm shift and the cosmic consequences of the resurrection. Yet to fathom it, to understand it? It comforts me that faith is deeper

Rainbow reflected in the fjord-side windows of the monastery.
All photos © Tautra Mariakloster. See also www.tautra.no and our Facebook page.

Taken from the side of the monastery in winter.

Taken very early in the morning when a remarkable gold light
bathed the whole southern end of the island.

Usually when we see the Aurora Borealis from Tautra, it is a low green
bow. This night, however, we were treated to a more spectacular
display.

The pattern of light and shadow from our glass roof over First Choir.

October light on the mountains across the fjord.

There are two seagull chicks hidden in these photos. Can you see them?

Frostrøyk occurs when warmer air hits the colder fjord and the condensation forms "frost smoke."

Compline in the winter darkness.

Sr. Rafael in our refectory, where we sit at one long table so we all have a view of the fjord.

Taken from the back of the monastery in winter.

Dramatic "firecloud" sunset.

Dramatic summer storm over the fjord.

Pattern of light on the crucifix in the cloister.

Tautra Mariakloster's 20th anniversary, March 25, 2019:
Sr. Anne, Sr. Agnes, Sr. Rafael, Sr. Gilchrist, Sr. Christina, Sr. Hanne-Maria,
Sr. Rosemary, Sr. Marjoe, Sr. Brigitte, Sr. Anne Elizabeth, Sr. Lisbeth,
Sr. Renata, Sr. Sheryl.

than understanding. We believe it, and we can grow more and more in this faith, with or without understanding. I can wonder at the sight of the beautiful spider with a cross on its back, and its webs, the beauty and complexity of both the spider and its work, even if I don't understand the full meaning of the spider's role in nature.

July 23 is the feast of one of Europe's patrons, the Swedish Saint Brigitte, and the feast day of our prioress. We are celebrating with a short-distance outing to our newly bought cabin at the shore of our property. Although it is only a two-minute walk down there, it has a character of being a secluded space, and especially so on the fjord side, where you have just the water and the other side of the fjord in front of you. At high tide the water is only a few yards from the walls. Celebrating the feast of the prioress has something in common with the queen's birthday: It is celebrating one who represents the unity of the community. For us Christians a king or queen or a leader or ruler is a servant more than a person of power. Looking at the medieval crucifix in the Munkeby chapel, it strikes me that Christ is King, what it is to rule from the cross: being nailed, so you cannot move hands or feet, hanging in terrible pain and weakness. This is the deep unity of heaven and earth, this is how Jesus is one with us and one with the Father.

The text of several of the antiphons for Saint Brigitte in our liturgy comes from her *Revelations*:[1]

Be humble as I am humble, says the bridegroom; so will your heart be with my heart, burning with love for me.

Love only me, and you shall receive all that you want in abundance.

The Lauds and Vespers antiphons are all about Wisdom. Saint Brigitte (+1373) was a mother of eight children and founder of a religious order. A brave woman, she admonished the exiled pope to return to Rome. The *Blåkyrkan*, "The Blue

---

[1] See, e.g., *The Revelations of St. Birgitta of Sweden*, trans. Denis Searby, intro. and notes Bridget Morris (New York: Oxford University Press, 2006).

Church" built according to her Revelations, has two equal naves, one for the nuns and one for the monks. In connection with Pope John Paul II's visit to Scandinavia in 1989, an ecumenical Mass was held in this Vadstena Church, and the Eucharist was celebrated simultaneously in the Catholic and Lutheran rite at different altars in the two parallel naves. This memory stays with me as a hope for the future unity of Christians.

This last week of July we move from one feast to another. The 25th is Saint James, one of the sons of Zebedee, whom Jesus gave the name Sons of Thunder. He is one of the three apostles closest to Jesus, and thus closest to us. Why did Jesus choose these three to be closer to him than the others? Simply because we need leaders among leaders? The gospels portray James as an ambitious leader type. Often he is shown as not understanding what Jesus was about. What about us?

The feast of Saints Joachim and Anne is the feast day of our sisters Anne Elizabeth and Anne. We celebrate the grandparents of Jesus with a coffee break after Mass. Grandparents are generous, and we enjoy the cookies we get on their behalf. The day is filled with prayers and gratitude for our sisters, and for our grandparents.

July 28, the eve of *Olsok*, the Solemnity of Saint Olav, Norway's patron saint and Eternal King. Two busloads of Catholic pilgrims are visiting us on their way to Munkeby. This year they will have Mass at Munkeby and stop here only for Sext and a coffee break. Sr. Lisbeth has made her best chocolate chip cookies. We receive the visitors in the visitor center after the prayer, serving homemade red currant juice, coffee, and tea. It is a short visit with short exchanges, but they are so grateful. Grateful to see us, greet us, pray with us in our beautiful church, and be confirmed about the monastic presence in Norway.

The pilgrimage to Stiklestad, where Saint Olav was martyred in 1030, is normally on Sunday. A carload of us will go for the two-kilometer procession to the medieval church built over the place where he was slain in battle. It is a small group of

Catholics walking along the golden barley fields, singing and praying the rosary. Yet we almost fill the church graciously lent to us by the Lutheran parish. It touches our deep Christian roots, praying here where our people killed our king, who gave his life to Christ. His death became a turning point for Christianity in our country. Through his death the death of Christ became real and present to the Norwegians. This yearly visit means coming back to the mystery of the cross here on our own soil in our tough climate.

On the solemnity itself, July 29, we rent a bus and all go to Trondheim for the Catholic Mass in the medieval cathedral, which is now the Lutheran cathedral. Saint Olav is buried here, but his grave has not been known since it was hidden some sixty years after the Reformation. You clearly sense the holiness of this place, a cathedral from the twelfth century, with remains of the church built in the 1060s.

Celebrating Mass in this Gothic cathedral, which is the heart of Norway, opens so many aspects of our history and communion with generations before us. It has been an important European shrine all these centuries, so it is a special connection with the universal Church. The sanctuary is built with the same dimensions as the Church of the Holy Sepulcher in Jerusalem, and as a replica of the sanctuary of Saint Thomas Becket in Canterbury. Saint Thomas was a friend of our archbishop, Saint Eystein, the main builder of our twelfth-century cathedral; he also built a chapter house inspired by the Cistercians. He himself testified to a miracle Saint Olav worked with a boy from the household of Munkeby before 1180.

"The Lord is great and worthy to be praised. He who through Saint Olav built a city in the North." This is how we start Vigils for the solemnity. Through the day we sing repeatedly: *Pray for us, Saint Olav, Eternal King of Norway, you who christened the people and the country, Christ's servant, Saint Olav. Pray for us, Saint Olav, Eternal King of Norway!*

In October we celebrate his conversion and baptism. It makes me humble to see what God can do through the baptism of one person, a Viking king, who was still very much a child of his brutal time. Yet he grew into an understanding of Christ that became more important than his own interests. His work introducing Christian laws and ethics gave the name to all Christian laws for the next centuries in our country, The Law of Saint Olav. The way he gave his own life in death was seen as a sign of martyrdom, and through the centuries he has been and is venerated in many countries for his help and healing. We entrust our people to his care, that he will once again show us the way to Christ.

July

Summer, summer, summer
Nights without darkness
Days without nights
No stars, no moon

Warm, kind air
Welcome breeze
Clover scent
Rose scent
Manure scent
Newly cut green grass

Saint Olav, our King, our friend,
Leader, Christ's beloved lawgiver
His corpse smelling of roses
One single Christian life
Still bearing fruit,
hope and direction.

Berries and Martyrs

Sr. Hanne-Maria Berentzen, OCSO

Dark velvet night
Soft and warm
Warm like southern life
Whimsy bats in the air
Hot coffee
ten minutes before Vigils

The first movements of the morning
White light on the eastern sky
Aspen leaves dancing
Singing
Only in the top of the tree
Only one tree towards the west
A northern tree plays in
Soft morning aspen music
Before the fjord starts singing

The newness of an August day
Once again the night was night
Light coming only with the day
Summer passing.

August is golden and red. Golden barley fields, red berries, and the blood of the martyrs. August is soft velvet darkness and a glowing full moon hanging over the southern mountains behind the fjord. August is the link between summer and fall. August has everything.

For us the peak of the summer is July 29, *Olsok*: the solemnity of Saint Olav. Nature, climate, liturgy, business, and life in the community are all woven into this rhythm. The summer is before and after Olsok.

August has its kick-off with Saint Olav. This is when our berry season starts, with the first big, red raspberries. Yes, July has the strawberries, but we have just a few plants of those. A couple of sisters love to contemplate the field of strawberries and bring home from the woods a pint or two whenever we have time for this luxury of tiny fingernail-size fruits of Paradise. The *community* berry season starts with Saint Olav and the raspberries.

Once the raspberries start, they ask for love on a daily basis. Then they love back. We have three patches. Sr. Rosemary is in charge of the oldest, in the old orchard. They need to be picked every day for about three weeks, then every other day for a few more weeks. I am in charge of the patch by the cemetery, closer to the fjord, where the climate is tougher. We both try to check the one row by the vegetable garden. Luckily, God is sending us good volunteers every summer. If we think we are short of them when August comes, then suddenly a former volunteer will ask if she or he can come for a few weeks. Nothing is better than those who already know the ropes of Tautra life and can enter right into the rhythm without instruction.

Our community is slowly but steadily growing. The guesthouse is often filled to overflowing during the summer. We may be twenty-five or thirty for dinner, with fresh raspberries for dessert, not once but several times, and for breakfast, sometimes also for supper. We also fill a whole freezer with raspberries. They will last us until the feast of Saint Olav next year, when the new berries are ready to be picked.

The Historic Market outside the Nidaros Cathedral in Trondheim ends in the first week of August. The old *Translatio* of Saint Olav, August 3, is not on our liturgical calendar but is still there in the quiet background. Saint Olav follows us also when we move on to the other side of the peak of the summer. The Historic Market normally covers about a quarter of our yearly sales of soaps, balms, and creams. Saint Olav himself is helping with our economy.

The Church has omitted the celebration of the *translatio* of saints, the day when the dead was proclaimed a saint and enshrined. With the hosts of saints we may celebrate, I understand the need for simplification. Yet I like to take a new look at the meaning of the *translatio*.

In a secularized society, people no longer understand our relation to the saints and why we need them. One year the theme for the official (Lutheran) festival of Saint Olav was Saint Olav as an *idol*. An idol is the opposite of a Christian saint. Focusing on the *translatio* may help us understand the meaning of declaring a person a saint. It is not to show an impeccable life totally different from ours; rather, it is that person's role in transmitting the Gospel that is important, how the example of the saint can help us to a deeper understanding of the mystery of the incarnation.

Was it Saint Olav who made August the month of martyrs for me? Or the fact that August is kicked off by Saint Olav and ends with Saint John the Baptist, whose name I received and whom I have chosen as my patron saint? Is it the Feast of the Transfiguration, clearly showing that the Glory of Christ is his suffering and his cross? Or is it Saint Lawrence, Saint Theresa Benedicta of the Cross, and Saint Maximilian Kolbe?

Maybe it is everything. Even the summer, the berries, and the night. Maybe it is my retreat, that breathing space that opens up for me a deeper awareness of the wholeness of our life, of how everything *is* our life.

Saint Olav plays an important role in my life. He has been there as long as I can remember. When I was a child, we spent the summer in our cabin outside Sandefjord, a city south of Oslo. All the cabin families made a big bonfire on the shore and celebrated the feast of Saint Olav. In those days, it was a public holiday in that county.

I was four or five years old when my father showed me the ancient rock outside our medieval church in Oddernes with an inscription in runes, the old Norse alphabet, saying "Eivind,

King Olav's godson, built this church on his ancestral ground."
This close connection with the sacred in our daily life and with
Saint Olav has always followed me. He was the one who made
the difference in the christening of our country, and for this I
am ever grateful. Visiting the Nidaros Cathedral in Trondheim
at the age of thirteen made a deep impression on me. Here I
touched the heart of Norway, a center of European culture, the
Gothic cathedrals, and the rich symbolism of the Catholic faith.
No Lutheran anti-saint propaganda could change my relationship with Saint Olav. Later he himself led me to the Catholic
Church.

When I entered Cistercian monastic life at Mount St. Mary's
Abbey in Wrentham, Massachusetts, I knew that the privilege
of being called to this life was a gift and a challenge from Saint
Olav. It was a vocation for my people, no matter where I lived.
Six years later I was called to be part of the foundation at Tautra
made by Our Lady of the Mississippi Abbey. My call is to learn
from the martyrs this total gift of self.

Several years ago I was invited to make my retreat at a
mountain farm of some good friends. Since then Saint Olav
has guided my retreats in a graphic way. The farm *Fokstugu* is
one of four mountain farms first built by King Øystein in the
late twelfth century to secure the journey over the Dovre
mountains for pilgrims going to the shrine of Saint Olav in
Nidaros (the old name of Trondheim). In the 1990s the Norwegian government took the initiative of marking the paths
to Nidaros, opening them again for the pilgrims. Our friends
made their farm into a pilgrim center, with a small chapel
where they pray Lauds and Compline every day. The Angelus
bell sings into the wilderness three times a day, summer and
winter.

Hiking through these mountains dividing the country into
north and south, I was guided by the cross of Saint Olav. The
blossoming cross, painted in red on slates and rocks all through
these majestic mountains, shows the path. It resonates with a
verse in our national anthem: "On this country Olav painted

the cross with his blood." If you carefully walk from cross to cross, you will get through the mountains safely. From cross to cross.

What fits better to a month when we celebrate the ascent of Jesus and his three disciples to Mount Tabor, where he made known to them that his coming passion would be his glory?

One year the whole community went with our brothers at Munkeby to one of the higher mountains in our area, with a fantastic view over our county. It was the feast of the Transfiguration, up on a mountain with Jesus. Just as we reached the top, happy to have some strong monks to help us up, and enjoying the breathtaking view, the clouds covered the mountain. For a few minutes we were enveloped in fog. A good experience of the Gospel for the day.

These last years I have made my retreat at our brothers' monastery, Munkeby. First I thought I would miss the mountain experience and the connection with Saint Olav and the crosses. With joy I discovered that Munkeby is situated right on the pilgrim routes between Stiklestad, where Olav was martyred, and Trondheim. The mountains are close, and I can reach the area by bike. In the landscape along the river and through the woods I had to be even more focused to see cross after cross and not go astray. The cross has preference over the straight path.

August 9 is the Feast of Saint Theresa Benedicta of the Cross, the Jewish philosopher Edith Stein, who is now a patron saint of Europe. Giving your life for your people is the theme of Saint Olav that always hits me. This is what she also did. She understood that she was dying as a martyr for Christ, with her Jewish people. With the persecution of Jews and Christians in Europe and all over the world today, we do not know when this might be asked of us as we follow Christ. We need the saints to remind us of this reality and prepare us for our cross, no matter what it may be.

The next day, August 10, we go back to the persecutions of the earliest centuries. Saint Lawrence, the archdeacon of Rome, was tortured to death under Caesar Valerian in 258, roasted on a grill, says the tradition. Like Saint Theresa Benedicta, he knew what was coming: his pope, Sixtus II, and four deacons had been killed four days before. Lawrence was asked to bring the treasures of the Church to Valerian. He distributed all he could to the poor and brought the poor, the widows, and the lepers to Caesar, saying, "Behold, here are the treasures of the Church."

What an example for us monks and nuns who have vowed a life of poverty! How do we do it in our day? This question is haunting me. To what radical poverty are we called? How are we in our wealthy societies called to become those treasures of the church, and to share what we have with the poor? How are we carrying the poor of the world today to our governments and our people?

May Saint Lawrence always challenge us to move closer to Christ and not to cling to our comfortable life of superfluity, which turns us away from suffering and danger. This too is grace, and it has to come from within, from the Holy Spirit moving our hearts.

With Maximilian Kolbe on August 13 we continue to move from martyr to martyr in our liturgy. Now we are back to recent history and another Nazi concentration camp, where he offered his life to save the life of a father of a family. Saint Olav, the Transfiguration, Saint Theresa Benedicta, Saint Lawrence, Saint Maximilian. They all remind me that this is what the incarnation means, this is the Gospel of Jesus. His life in us can grow so strong that we can go beyond. We can give our life, not only for a friend, but for somebody unknown.

These saints did it in their following of Christ. In the way they show us Christ, they dominate the spiritual sense of August.

Having the opportunity to take my retreat during this second week of August brings the message into my very body in a tangible way. Climbing the mountains of Dovre, taking a seven- or ten-hour hike every day, challenging my fear of steep mountains, walking step by step with Jesus into the wilderness, or biking the back roads of our own home area to reach Munkeby: the physical effort makes me understand why the evangelists underline that Jesus was taking the disciples up on a very high mountain. Using the body helps move into a deeper unity of body and soul, coming to a deeper understanding of the mystery of the incarnation. The gospels we read during this time in Year A repeatedly bring out that Jesus is really the Son of God, truly God and truly man. Reflecting on the mystery in adoration and prayer, biking and hiking, with the help of the martyrs, brings me to the stillness point within where nothing and everything matters. Where you can let go of everything.

Come August, and we know that the night is coming back. No real darkness yet, but the summer night is not as fair as before. Soon we will need the lights on for Vigils. For the Feast of the Assumption, August 15, Our Lady who has the moon under her feet, it is time to discover the moon shining golden in the dusk. During the summer months I have forgotten about the moon and the stars. I have not even noticed the white shadow in the sky now and then. We watch the tide as needed, but without regard to the position of the moon. With our rhythm of night and day we may still wait some days before we see the stars, but they will come. What a joy of new discovery! We forget many things during the light summer. Suddenly the Tautra lighthouse is blinking again when you look toward the eastern sky before Vigils, watching the dawn breaking. The farm lights across the fjord are lit; again we see the lights of the first cars with people on their way to work. An old hobby becomes new, distinguishing between the lights of the cars and the lights of the boats, learning to read the signs of the night. It can be as easy and difficult as a spiritual discernment.

August has two solemnities very dear to us Cistercians: The Assumption of Our Lady is the patronal feast of our Order. Five days later we celebrate our best-known Cistercian abbot, Saint Bernard of Clairvaux. They fit well together, as Saint Bernard had a deep love for Our Lady and wrote beautifully about her. She kept her mantle well around him and our whole

Order. The Assumption is full of joy and hope in the faith of
the resurrection, this hope that carries and sustains us on the
way between the Transfiguration and the Exaltation of the
Cross (September 14). The Virgin Mary always follows Christ
in the liturgy. In August, we celebrate the Dedication of the
Basilica Maria Maggiore on the day before the Transfiguration.
This important basilica in Rome was built in honor of Mary,
the Mother of God. It is as the Mother of God that we believe
she was the first fruit of the resurrection after her Son. A month
later, we will celebrate her sorrow at the death of Jesus. She is
our Mother in sorrow, joy, and hope. This joy comes to me daily
in passing my sisters in the cloister, the hallway, the kitchen,
and being greeted with a smile. A smile makes the difference
in a day.

As I have learned to love Saint Bernard, his love for Our
Lady has also drawn me closer to her.

The collection we have of Saint Bernard's letters contains a
letter to our Archbishop Eskild of Lund. He visited Clairvaux,
became a friend of Bernard's, and later entered Clairvaux. For
the celebration of Eskild's ordination as bishop in 1133, the
Scandinavian bishops probably discussed the new growing
order of Cîteaux. Within ten to fifteen years after he became
archbishop, Cistercian monasteries existed in all the dioceses of
the bishops who met in Lund. Lyse monastery outside Bergen,
the founding house of the medieval monastery at Tautra, was
one of them.

The first seven years on Tautra we celebrated the solemnity
of Saint Bernard with Mass in the ruins of our monastery on
Tautra (founded March 25, 1207), together with members of
our Support Group, the people who prayed our present monastery into being. I will always celebrate this feast in gratitude
for them. Without the Support Group, we wouldn't have been
at Tautra. It started at the feast of Saint Olav in 1991, when about
thirty-five people on retreat decided to pray every day for a
future Cistercian monastery in Norway. The Group quickly
grew to 100, later 150, 200, and more. Their friendship, prayer,

support, and practical and economic help are like foundation stones of our monastery. Ingerid was one of them. When she was buried on the Feast of Saint Bartholomew in 2017, she had been lighting a candle and praying for us every morning for twenty-six years. We enjoy the fruits of such faithful prayers.

August is berry time. There are still some field strawberries, my favorite teachers in the spiritual life: tiny, tiny. Sweet, shining red in the grass or the moss. Hidden among stinging nettles, thistles, and thorns, or under juniper berry bushes with sharp needles. Their utmost sweetness makes nothing of the pains to pick them. They are humble in their littleness, and it is a humble task to pick them. I must go down on my knees, and often stay there. Field strawberries are the berries of Paradise. We have lots of them on Tautra.

Picking raspberries is different. The bushes are tall, but you must bend for the lower branches. Some berries will call you to the bush, bright and red. Others will hide under broad leaves curling themselves protectively around the berries. You should ask each one if it is ready to give itself to you. If you force them, they are sour; if you respect their proper timing and reverence their free will, you get the sweetest and nicest fruits.

You must be there when the right time has come. If you miss it, they will rot and taste bad. This goes for all the berries. They are as different as the saints in our liturgical celebrations. With the raspberries come the yellow gooseberries, then the green gooseberries, then the red gooseberries, then the black currants. The red currants can wait if we put nets on the bushes. If we tarry with the nets, we may lose them. The starlings will come in flocks of fifty or a hundred. When they leave, the bush is not red any more. With nets on the bushes we can concentrate on the raspberries and take the currants when convenient.

August is still summer. The grass does not dry up so fast after the rain, but it is warm enough to go barefooted down to the fjord for an evening dip. It is the beauty of the northern parts of our country that nature is green all through the summer. Shortly after the second cutting of hay, the hayfields are green again. The lawns stay green until a heavy frost in the winter.

The barley fields around us are moving from green to yellow and golden at the feast of Saint Olav. One of the antiphons we use for the feast is "Unless the grain of wheat falls to the earth and dies, it remains just a grain of wheat. But if it dies, it produces much fruit" (John 12:24). Outside the monastery, you see the ears full of grain bowing their heads and becoming ready for the harvest. One morning we hear the reading from the Book of Ruth: "They arrived in Bethlehem at the beginning of the barley harvest" (Ruth 1:22). That very day our neighbor starts the barley harvest to the sound of migrating geese. In flocks of thirty or seventy, one hundred or five hundred, they take a rest here on their way south.

August is the time of radical change in the life of the Tautra bird sanctuary: the birds are leaving. No seagulls shouting through the night. The morning is quiet. Nobody cares when we go down to the shore. No chicks of the seagulls are flying out over the water with their dry squeaking baby voices. No grown gulls are crying out about the advancing dangers, no watchers flying up on the roof of the boathouses for an overview in protecting the chicks.

The children start school in mid-August. The seagull chicks start primary school a few weeks earlier. About ten of them gather on the lawn with one of the grownups. The older chicks are already in junior high by the causeway, soon ready to go to town for high school, and then off to Europe for the winter. By the time of the Assumption there are no fishing gulls to be heard or seen. The black-headed gulls are long gone, and the few families of terns with them. The oyster catchers gather on the long shallow beach in our bay. Within a week they are gone. No more hysteric concerts in the air, no parents teaching the youngsters how to be oyster catchers. The shore is quiet, except for the ugly cries of the herons in the early evening.

After five months of noisy seabirds making themselves heard, everything is quiet when I open the door towards the fjord in the early morning. Now the noise is on the other side of the monastery. The migrating geese start coming before the feast of Saint Olav. The monastery is not very big or very broad, but each side of the building presents itself as a different world. What is God giving right here at this particular moment? What is the fjord singing, and where is the singing coming from?

I never knew about singing waters until we came to Tautra. The special currents, the tide and the wind, make the water sing. Each day with a different song from a different place, beautiful and interesting.

After our morning Mass and chapter meeting, I take my cup of coffee on the southern side, enjoying two minutes of drinking the silence and the beauty of this sheltered reality. Often the sun lifts the morning. After the prayer of None, I choose the windy northern side, drinking the beauty of the fjord, ever moving, ever reflecting the changing sky.

One clear morning I hear a big group of barn swallows all crying out in the same way, flying high in a circle. They are flying more individually than other birds. Yet they are clearly together, doing the same thing. Suddenly they stop crying out and scatter themselves over a larger area, still flying high, but now quietly. After a few minutes, some start making the normal swallow sounds. Then quiet again. For several minutes, there is no sound. As on a signal, they gather again as I first saw them, all crying out in the same chick sound, practicing for the long journey southwards. I love their elegant, yet flimsy flight. Is this how the angels fly, soaring more than flying, carried by the unseen draft and wind?

It reminds me of our community scattered around the house and the garden, each doing her own thing. When the bell rings us to prayer, we all gather in the chapel, singing the same songs of praise. Not always with one voice, but we are growing into greater unity.

The swallow chicks start school when the children do, learning the balance between individuality and common life in their flight, and how to land and sit together. It is fun to watch them—one group landing in a row on the roof of our offices. That is the easiest, with a low angle on the copper roof, and not so difficult to get all the way up to sit. More demanding is the slippery church roof of glass and steel. This is for the chicks of the first litter. You recognize the difference between first and second year novices settling into the community and learning the monastic way of daily life.

Singing birds and the screaming birds, a variety of sounds for each kind. Chicks and adults have different voices and sounds. Living a life of prayer and praise, singing the praise of God seven times a day, plus Mass, I feel connected with other creatures who do the same. Do the swallows, starlings, and seagulls notice the same? They often join us in our singing, sitting on the roof or the cross of the bell tower.

Working in the office one morning I become aware of birds having their second breakfast on the lawn. The starling chicks with their shining white spots, the wagtail chicks with their still downy heads and not yet black plumage, only different shades of grey. The swallow chicks flying low although the barometer would tell them otherwise. A starling chick is bowing his head to avoid colliding with the swallow flying high speed right over his head. It's like a schoolyard where children are teasing and challenging one another. Or like the challenges of a novitiate with sisters from very different cultures learning to blend—from England, Poland, Belgium, Vietnam, France . . . .

One day I hear a big bang in my cell. There are three tiny down feathers on my window, and on the grass below, I see two brambling chicks who did not know what a window was. One is already dead. The other one is breathing, eyes open, but in shock. One wing still spread out. I decide not to shock it more by going out to rescue it. The cats seldom come here at this time, and the big birds will not come so close to the wall. I check again after ten minutes. He has pulled in his wing, still breathing, still both eyes open, still in shock. Fifteen minutes later his head is under the wing. He is sleeping. After None the little bird is gone. I go out, taking the dead bird to rest a different place. You don't forget the beauty of these small birds. None of them falls to the ground without our heavenly Father's knowledge.

The bramblings come only in August and September, in big flocks on their way somewhere. They love our aronia berries. The chicks have not learned to fear humans yet, so I can study them close up. The birds play an important role in our life in a bird sanctuary. We enjoy their seasonal behavior, coming and going, calling and breeding.

One early morning a golden plover is calling. No answer. It reminds me of the mountains where I always hear this calling—with answers. August gives a sense of the mountains. We may have those wonderful, warm days when the new darkness is velvet soft, the bats are out, and it could just as well be in Italy. Then we have the cool draft and sharp air telling about Fall coming and explaining why so many birds are leaving. The golden plover belongs to May and August. There is one particular flock of thirty or forty birds that come to rest here for a few weeks during migration. The lonely bird this morning—is it a forerunner, or is it one left behind?

It could be both, one left behind who becomes a forerunner. That is how the story of the Spencer community in Massachusetts started—a monk who was left behind and eventually became the forerunner of a new community in the US. Having come on a regular foundation to Norway, I love the stories of irregularity, showing how the Holy Spirit works through all our failures and weaknesses. The monk mentioned went shopping and missed the boat back to France.

What happens to the birds who missed the migration group? Will they make it? They need the support of the others on the journey. Just like us. The privilege of monastic life is this support of others in the prayer and singing of the Office, much like the singing and calling of the birds.

August is a season for concerts. The concerts of nature. Not only the singing of the fjord and the variation of the calling of the swallows. The beauty of the green trees and the green grass throughout the summer does not emphasize that fall is coming. But unless we have a lot of rain, August opens the concert of the aspen trees. The first little dryness changes the music of the aspen—it gets a crisper sound, and we know the summer is fading.

When the darkness comes back, the early morning changes. During the summer, the sun is up before us. Now we experience the night, the dawn, and the daybreak. The fact that it is not always so makes the experience new, entering into the mystery of creation, being present when God starts creating a new day. First I can see what is mountains, what is sky, and what is fjord. When the eastern sky lightens up, the aspen leaves start shivering. A short melody in one tree, then a short melody in another tree. Then total stillness and total silence before the sunrise breeze comes in full strength. The day has become day.

The starlings give the evening concert. They are in high school already, flying over a larger area. When they come, they bring the whole school and the school choir, landing in the old ash tree by the guesthouses. The variety in the song of more than a hundred birds is like the choir of saints. They fly in tight form, close to one another, and in high speed. How come they don't collide? Like a host of angels, every movement is done in unison. Is eternity when we become united like that?

No month is like August when it comes to berries. Our August breakfasts are the best. We can eat fresh berries at will—raspberries, red currants, and black currants.

Good neighbors in advanced age also invite us to harvest from their abundance. Their garden is a paradise, much warmer than ours, and with a beautiful view. We go there, enjoy picking the shiny, red currants, enjoy not being able to finish one bush in the afternoon. They will last us another month. A month inviting for red currant juice, jam, and a French pie with vanilla cream.

As plentiful as the berries are the choice readings we have at Vigils from the pen of Saint Augustine. The memorials of his death and the death of his mother Monica on the following day give good reason for thanksgiving. Year after year we hear the same readings explaining the meaning of the Scriptures, and like the *lectio divina* of Holy Scripture itself, his words come to me fresh and new, no matter how well I think I know them:

> Urged to reflect upon myself, I entered under your guidance into the inmost depth of my soul. I was able to do so because you were my helper. On entering into myself I saw, as it were with the eye of the soul, what was beyond the eye of the soul, beyond my spirit: your immutable light. It was not the ordinary light perceptible to all flesh, nor was it merely something of greater magnitude, but still essentially akin, shining more clearly and diffusing itself everywhere by its intensity. No, it was something entirely distinct, something altogether different from all these things; and it did not rest above my mind as oil on the surface of water, nor was it above me as heaven is above earth. This light was above me because it had made me; I was below it because I was created by it. He who has come to know the truth knows this light.[1]

Our summer starts by celebrating the birth of Saint John the Baptist, and it ends with the celebration of his death. He was the forerunner. As his conception and his life pointed to Christ, so did his death as a martyr for Truth point to the death of Jesus on the cross. The red raspberries are picked, but there are still bushes shining red with currants.

The martyr who was forerunner of Christ points to martyrs of all ages, those who, like him, realized the depth of Grace and Truth.

How do *we* live our lives pointing to Christ?

---

[1] Augustine, *Confessions* 7.10.18 (CSEL 33:157–63).

September

Looking for the Next Cross

Sr. Sheryl Frances Chen, OCSO

Plums. Small purple spherical plums. Oval yellow plums. Juicy red-orange Victoria plums. Small green plums. Round blue "Opal" plums. September is the month for plums. The property on which the guesthouse stands came with its own orchard: several varieties of apples and plums, and berry bushes: large raspberries (don't touch the branches or you will receive a reprimand from Sr. Rosemary!), red currants, black currants, gooseberries. Fortunately they don't all ripen at the same time, but the month of September is busy with our little harvest.

Of course we can't eat all of it fresh. Many an afternoon is spent with several sisters and volunteers pitting plums and freezing them for lovely desserts during the winter, and peeling apples and making applesauce. Sr. Rosemary carefully freezes our raspberries, standing them in rows on a baking sheet; only after they are individually frozen does she place them in two-liter ice cream boxes in the freezer. They not only maintain their shape better this way when they are thawed, but they retain more flavor as well. We can make it from one season to the next eating only our own fruit on memorials (no dessert at all on ferial days). What a treat to have our own raspberries over creamy, Norwegian (because the cows are so happy) ice cream on a feast day in the winter!

But back to plums. When it's a good year for plums, all our neighbors, and it seems everyone on Frosta, has an abundance of plums, so much that none of us can process it all. But no one wants the crop to be wasted either. We pit and freeze, pit and freeze, until our fingers can hardly function anymore. One day while we prayed midafternoon prayer, someone came to our door, set down a large boxful of ripe plums, and departed without letting us know they had been there. We discovered the plums only when we came out of church after prayer. Oh, no! MORE plums! We really had enough of our own. But what a good idea! We could just deliver boxfuls of plums to our neighbors when they weren't home and sneak away!

The abundance of the harvest is juxtaposed with the middle of the month, September 14, the feast of the Triumph of the Cross, which marks the beginning of the monastic fast. It used to be the day on which the general chapter of our Order began, every year, at Cîteaux. From September 14 until Easter, except in Christmastime, we have only soup and bread for our dinner on Fridays. In Lent, we do the same on Wednesdays as well. September 14, 2009, was the opening of Munkeby Mariakloster, the home of our Cistercian brothers from Cîteaux who live in Levanger, an hour's drive north of Tautra. In his homily on that historic day, Dom Olivier, abbot of Cîteaux, cited Saint Bernard: *Ordo nostrae crux est.* Our Order is the cross.

The cross and Jesus crucified are central to our Order. Everything revolves around this salvific event: "For his sake I have accepted the loss of all things, and I consider them so much rubbish, that I may gain Christ and be found in him, . . . depending on faith to know him and the power of his resurrection and sharing of his sufferings by being conformed to his death" (Phil 3:8-10 NAB).

What does it mean in daily life to share Christ's sufferings in a way that is redemptive? In September, the gospel "Deny yourself and take up your cross" (Matt 16:24) is also proclaimed. Br. Ronnie Fogarty used this verse in the context of emotional maturity. It's hard work to deny our instinctive defense mechanisms and other neurotic ways of dealing with reality, and to take up the discipline of carrying the cross of owning our own emotions and not projecting them onto others. Fr. Steve Rossetti, another psychologist who gives us yearly input, says ninety percent of what we think others are thinking is a projection of our own thoughts.

In our international community, with sisters from eight countries, we each experience the cross in a different way when what is most precious to us is crucified. Or at least it may feel as though it is dying on a cross. It could be giving up my own country, or the food that I am used to, or the possibility of getting a job and helping the people in my country. It may be giving up other customs from my upbringing, even certain treats or special celebrations that I am used to. The Rule says that when we are clothed, we put off our own things and put on the things of the monastery. We wear the clothes we are given and are not to complain about the color or coarseness. There is a basic openness to receiving here that I think Benedict wants us to have as a fundamental attitude. Monastic life, says Br. Cyril, one of the founders of Munkeby, is about learning to receive. Before we let the complaint out of our mouth, we should try the discipline of asking God what he wants us to receive in this situation, at this moment. Often we are so busy objecting that we miss the grace being given.

Bishop Robert Barron, in a DVD series on Catholicism, reminds us that the last recorded words of Mary are "Do whatever he tells you."[1] I think we often forget to ask God "What do *you* want me to do?" We have a tendency to ask ourselves, "what do *we* want to do?"—about giving to charity or about having dessert in the refectory, for instance. But do we really ask, every moment of every day, what do *you* want me to do? God wants us to take up our own particular cross, each day. What needs to be crucified in us will probably change over time if we are serious about going deeper and being crucified with Christ.

[1] Robert Barron, *Catholicism: The Pivotal Players* (Word on Fire Catholic Ministries), 2016.

In the beginning it may be easy to see the many sacrifices that need to be made to enter a monastic community and go through at least five and a half years of formation. We hope it is not an end of conversion but a good beginning. Later in life it takes constant vigilance to keep attentive to God, to keep asking what we need to do to carry out the divine will and not presume that we have become so close to God that our will is the same as God's.

Author and rabbi Chaim Potok wrote that Jews do not have a symbol, like the crucifixion, for ultimate desolation. That is what we are called to! And that is our glory. The name of the feast is the Triumph of the Cross. This sign of ultimate abandonment becomes the sign of ultimate triumph and victory over death. Originally the feast was called the Finding of the True Cross. In 326 Saint Helena discovered the true cross in Jerusalem. In 335 the emperor Constantine dedicated the Church of the Holy Sepulcher on September 14. In 614 the Persians stole the cross, and in 629 it was recovered and brought back on September 14.

The finding of the true cross. That's interesting. Maybe we have to discover and find the treasure that is hidden in each cross we experience. Maybe someone has to reveal it for us. We find the treasure of a tiny piece of wood that has been redemptive and has brought new life. What are the tiny pieces of wood in our own life, little or big deaths, that have brought us new life when we have had the courage to embrace it? That's what we do every Good Friday when we have the ceremony of the adoration of the cross. It's the wood that bore our Savior. There's not supposed to be a corpus on it. We kiss the wood that carried Jesus, after he had carried it and been nailed to it. When a sister does something that irritates me and it is a crucifixion of my tongue not to slice her with my words, do I find the treasure of the splinter and dare to kiss it, thanking God for the grace he wants to give me through that cross?

When we are going through something difficult, do we pray for it to *go away*, or do we ask to *go deeper*? Is God asking us to experience *failure* in this instance (so we learn to depend on him and not on ourselves), or is he asking us to experience a growth in *faith*? We can learn a lot about how closely we are following Jesus by observing our own reactions. When another sister or a guest or a volunteer leaves a mess, is my first reaction to judge and condemn her, or is it to think kindly of her and respond with an expression of mercy? If it's not mercy, I am not yet taking up my cross and following Jesus. Our former abbot general Dom Bernardo Olivera used to say, "If the wounds of another arouse your impatience and not your compassion, it is a sign that you have not yet accepted your own wounds."

My own Cistercian vocation was confirmed when I discovered twelfth-century abbot Guerric of Igny's sermons for Palm Sunday. His first sermon introduces the theme of *imitatio Christi* and his exhortation to enter Christ's wounds by contemplating them. He quotes Galatians 6:2, "Bear one another's burdens, and so you will fulfill the law of Christ,"[2] which Saint Benedict echoes in chapter 72 of his Rule. We bear one another's burdens, or, as one translation has it, we bear patiently with one another's defects, whether of body or behavior[3]—in short, we bear one another's wounds.

Guerric's second sermon for Palm Sunday focuses on being fastened to the cross together with Christ. He asks, "What so kindles the affections of the faithful, . . . what is there that so does sins to death, crucifies vices, nourishes and strengthens virtues as the remembrance of the Crucified?"[4] Contemplating Jesus Christ crucified aids both in eliminating vices and in

---

[2] Guerric of Igny, Sermon 29.1 (First Sermon for Palm Sunday), *Liturgical Sermons*, trans. The Monks of Mount Saint Bernard Abbey, CF 32 (Kalamazoo, MI: Cistercian Publications, 1971), 56.

[3] *RB 1980*, ed. and trans. Timothy Fry (Collegeville, MN: Liturgical Press, 1981), 295: "supporting with the greatest patience one another's weaknesses of body or behavior."

[4] Guerric, Sermon 30.1 (CF 32:59).

acquiring virtue: "Truly if you are fastened to the Cross together with Christ you are wise, you are just, you are holy, you
are free."[5] In listing four virtues, Guerric implies the four
dimensions of the cross. This allegorizing of the cross appears
also in medieval illustrations of the passion. Guerric continues:
"you who wisely glory, glory in your Lord's cross; its triumph
has set you free, its mystery has brought you life, its example
has justified you, its sign fortifies you."[6] Four benefits come
from the four dimensions of the cross:

> those who mark their foreheads with the sign of the cross
> to fortify themselves should mark their behavior with the
> example of the Crucified to justify themselves, living by
> the law of the cross as they are armed by faith in it. Other-
> wise it is mockery for the soldier to wear the badge of a
> king whose command he does not follow; it is wrong for
> him to protect himself with the sign of him whose bidding
> he does not obey.[7]

In the Prologue of the Rule, Saint Benedict bids the monk take
up the "strong and noble weapons of obedience"—these are
the same *arma Christi* that Guerric says arm one with the cross.
He says "the fear of God, like nails driven deep, fastens us to
the cross."[8] According to Saint Benedict, the fear of God is the
first step of humility.[9]

Further, Guerric bids us hang on the voluntary cross of peni-
tence until evening, that is, until the end of our life, in imitation
of Christ's example of persevering on the cross and not being
taken down from the cross before evening. So we imitate Christ
by crucifying our vices and hanging with him on our crosses

---

[5] Guerric, Sermon 30.1 (CF 32:60).
[6] Guerric, Sermon 30.4 (CF 32:62).
[7] Guerric, Sermon 30.4 (CF 32:62).
[8] Guerric, Sermon 30.5 (CF 32:63).
[9] RB 7.10 (*RB 1980*, 92).

all day, until the sacrifice is consummated in union with his own sacrifice. Then we do it again the next day, and the next, until the evening of our life. Guerric says that if we are the companions of Jesus' passion and glory, we take with us the sign of the cross, "the dying state of Jesus which you carry around in your body" (2 Cor 4:10).[10]

Guerric's third sermon for Palm Sunday uses the image of those who looked upon the bronze serpent in the desert and were healed: "as soon as the Lord looked upon Peter, Peter received from the graciousness of his most loving countenance the late rain, tears after sin."[11] This is the power of looking, of contemplation, of the gaze of those who love. Peter was wounded by a single glance of Jesus.

One of the key allusions in these sermons and in medieval art is Song 4:9: "You have wounded my heart, my sister, my bride, you have wounded my heart with a single glance of your eye." In the exchange of love in the Song of Songs there is a mutual wounding between the bride and the bridegroom.[12] The gaze of contemplation wounds the Spouse by a single glance. The soul and Christ wound each other, that is, pierce each other's heart, by contemplating each other in love. And that penetrating glance brings healing.

Guerric, in his fourth sermon for Palm Sunday, interprets the clefts of the rock in Song 2:14 ("O my dove in the clefts of the rock, let me hear your voice") as the wounds of Christ:

> Blessed is he who, in order that I might be able to build a nest in the clefts of the rock, allowed his hands, feet and side to be pierced and opened himself to me wholly that I might enter . . . and be protected in its recesses. The

[10] Guerric, Sermon 30.6 (CF 32:65).

[11] Guerric, Sermon 31.5 (CF 32:72).

[12] I have written previously on this mutual wound of love in the Cistercian fathers and mothers in my article, "Bernard's Prayer Before the Crucifix that Embraced Him: Cistercians and Devotion to the Wounds of Christ," CSQ 29 (1994): 23–54.

rock is a convenient refuge for the badgers,[13] but it is also
a welcome dwelling-place for the doves. These clefts, so
many open wounds all over his body, offer pardon to the
guilty and bestow grace on the just. Indeed it is a safe
dwelling place . . . to linger in the wounds of Christ, the
Lord, by devout and constant meditation.[14]

Christ's wounds are our entrance into his heart, and we dwell
there by contemplation:

> Go into the rock, then, man; hide in the dug ground. Make
> the Crucified your hiding place. He is the rock, he is the
> ground, he who is God and man. He is the cleft rock, the
> dug ground, for "they have dug my hands and my feet."
> Hide in the dug ground from the fear of the Lord, that is,
> from him fly to him, from the Judge to the Redeemer,
> from the tribunal to the Cross, from the Just One to the
> Merciful, from him who will strike the earth with the rod
> of his mouth to him who inebriates the earth with the
> drops of his blood, from him who will kill the godless
> with the breath of his lips to him who with the blood of
> his wounds gives life to the dead. Rather do not fly only
> to him but into him, go into the clefts of the rock, hide in
> dug ground, hide yourself in the very hands that were
> cleft, in the side that was dug. For what is the wound in
> Christ's side but a door in the side of the Ark for those
> who are to be saved from the flood?[15]

---

[13] Sr. Emmanuel Cazabonne, from the Abbey of Igny, told me that there
are no badgers left now, but there were many in France in the past. I was
curious about this image of contemplatives as badgers and discovered that
badgers are gregarious, nocturnal, live in groups in an extensive network of
burrows, and are known for their burrowing ability to dig for food—an apt
description of Cistercians living in community and burrowing into Scripture
during the early morning hours of darkness, digging for spiritual food.

[14] Guerric, Sermon 32.5 (CF 32:77).

[15] Guerric, Sermon 32.5: *Ingredere igitur in petra, o homo; abscondere in fossa
humo; pone tibi latibulum in crucifixo* (CF 32:77–78). The verb *abscondere* brings
to mind the *Anima Christi*, well loved as a prayer one prays after receiving

Guerric continues: "From the remembrance or the imitation of his passion, from meditation on his wounds, a pleasing voice sounds in the ears of the Bridegroom as if from the clefts of the rock. Now you, my brethren, have built your nests the more deeply within the clefts of the rock the more secretly you live in Christ and your life is hidden with Christ in God."[16] Guerric urges his monks to please the Bridegroom by imitating his passion and by dwelling in the wounds by meditation.

In allowing myself to be wounded, to continue to hold myself vulnerable to the difficulties of community life, I am imitating Christ. More than that, if I can imitate Christ exposed on the cross, I may have the courage to expose my wounds to my sisters. As we can draw close to the heart of God and find union with God through his wounds, we can draw closer to one another and find a communion of charity by an exchange of life and blood through each other's wounds.

Contact with God often occurs at a wound, at a weak place, not where I am "holy." It is precisely where my life is falling apart that God meets me. God does not save me from the wound, but rather communes with me in it. He himself is a wounded healer, and a wounded lover. Guerric's teaching leads me to reverence my sisters' wounds with the same devotion as I would kiss Jesus' wounds on the cross.

These themes from Guerric's sermons could easily have been illustrated by drawings found in the medieval art categories of *Christ crucified by the virtues*, the *amplexus Bernardi*, and the *arma Christi*. The imitation of Christ and entering Christ's wounds by contemplation still attract Benedictines and Cistercians today. I make no claim to a grand theory of

---

the Body and Blood of Christ in Communion: "Soul of Christ, sanctify me; Body of Christ, save me; Blood of Christ, inebriate me; Water from the side of Christ, wash me; Passion of Christ, strengthen me; O good Jesus hear me; Within your wounds hide me; separated from you, let me never be; From the evil one protect me; At the hour of my death, call me; And close to you bid me; That with your saints, I may be praising you forever and ever. Amen."

[16] Guerric, Sermon 32.6 (CF 32:78–79).

cultural continuity, yet I find that the following images that allegorize the cross, focus on the passion of Christ, and grant preeminence to Jesus' heart and wounds still bear meaning across the centuries. Today community life is much influenced by the insights of psychology. We are all wounded, and we take care to become aware of what is going on in our hearts. It is no surprise, then, that Guerric's medieval sermons, and medieval contemporary art, continue to nourish our spirituality. We imitate and contemplate a wounded God.

Saint Bernard, at the end of *De Consideratione*, comments on Ephesians 3:18: "What is God? The length, the width, the height and the depth."[17] God's length is his eternity, God's width is his charity, God's height is his majesty, and God's depth is his wisdom. These four attributes call to mind the four dimensions of the cross. One genre of medieval art, Christ crucified by the virtues, seems to illustrate this allegorizing of the virtues engendered by the crucifixion.

Christ crucified by the virtues is found in a Cistercian psalter in Besançon. A large Christ on the cross dominates the illustration. *Obedientia* nails Christ's hand, while *humilitas* crouches at the foot of the cross and focuses intently while hammering a nail through Christ's feet.[18] It is *caritas*, wearing a crown, who thrusts the spear into Christ's side, while *ecclesia*, also crowned, holds a chalice aloft to catch the blood and water spurting from the wound. By changing the *sponsa* figure into *caritas*, the artist implies that it is love that wounds Jesus.

At Chełmno, Poland, the Cistercian nuns' choir from the mid-fourteenth century was decorated with thirty-two scenes from the Song in fresco. While the figures are not named, one scene appears to be *Christ crucified by the virtues*, with, presum-

---

[17] Bernard, *De Consideratione* 5.13.27–32 (SBOp 3.489–93); *Five Books on Consideration: Advice to a Pope*, trans. John D. Anderson and Elizabeth T. Kennan, CF 37 [Kalamazoo, MI: Cistercian Publications, 1976], 173–79).

[18] *Christ crucified by the virtues*, Psalter, Bibliothèque Municipale de Besançon, MS 54, fol. 15v.

ably, the *sponsa* thrusting the spear into Christ's heart.[19] The parallel would have been obvious to the nuns as they glanced around the choir at the scenes in fresco: if it was the virtues that crucified Christ, when we imitate Christ in his virtues, we will be crucified with him. The practice of the virtues in Cistercian/Christian life will nail you to the cross.

Jeffrey Hamburger, in his *Nuns as Artists*, examines a group of drawings produced at the Benedictine abbey of St. Walburg in Eichstätt around 1500.[20] One drawing, called *Symbolic Crucifixion*, depicts the life of Christ in three sections simultaneously: as a baby in the beginning (*anfang*), the preaching Christ (*das mitel*), and the crucifixion (*endt*). His mother Mary sits atop the cross, her own heart pierced by five swords, demonstrating her own *imitatio Christi*. The arms of the cross are labeled *mercy*, *love*, and *justice*. The virtues surrounding the babe in swaddling clothes are poverty, suffering, and humility; the virtues operative in the middle of Christ's life are tenderness, unity, and temperance; and the virtues at the foot of the cross are forbearance, patience, and obedience. The anonymous nun artist implies that Christ suffered from the first moment of his appearance in human flesh, and that the virtues he practiced during his whole life were a lifelong crucifixion. The nuns of St. Walburg Abbey would also have seen their practice of the virtues required in living Benedictine community life as a lifelong crucifixion.

A stained-glass window depicting *Christ crucified by the virtues* in the Cistercian convent of Wienhausen in Lower Saxony, dating from ca. 1330, has the unique feature of Christ embracing *karitas* as she pierces his heart. The figures above the crossbeam are *justicia* and *pax*, while those at the foot of the cross

---

[19] Christ crucified by the virtues, Chelmno, nuns' choir (photo: Pracownia Fotograficzna PKZ w Toruniu/Stanislaw Resziewicz), Figure 8.6 in Jeffrey F. Hamburger, *The Visual and the Visionary: Art and Female Spirituality in Late Medieval Germany* (New York: Zone Books, 1998), 409–10.

[20] Jeffrey Hamburger, *Nuns as Artists: The Visual Culture of a Medieval Convent* (Berkeley: University of California Press, 1997), 102–38, fig. 66 B&W, plate 9, color, fol. 134.

are *misericordia* and *veritas*. Mary and John flank the Crucified. *Karitas* thrusts a dagger into Christ's heart as her left arm encircles his neck. Christ detaches his right arm from the cross to embrace *karitas* as she wounds him, as if thanking *karitas* for her heart-piercing devotion. The window depicts the mutual wounding and exchange of embraces between the bride and the bridegroom in the Song of Songs. The window indicates that it is desirable to imitate Christ in his being crucified by the virtues, and the Crucified rewards the charity that wounds his heart with an embrace.

The Wienhausen window with its Crucified detaching one of his arms to effect an embrace illustrates the genre of the *amplexus Bernardi*. The story of the Crucified embracing Saint Bernard is told in Conrad von Eberbach's *Exordium magnum cisterciense*:

> [A certain monk] once discovered the blessed Abbot Bernard praying alone in the church. While he was prostrate before the altar, there appeared placed on the floor before him a cross with its crucified, which the most blessed man adored and kissed most devoutly. Next that Majesty was seen to separate his arms from the branches of the cross to embrace and draw close the servant of God.[21]

The well-known "Christo Abrazado a San Bernardo" by Ribalta (1628) implies that Christ rests his weight on the *patibulum*, since his feet are still nailed as he detaches both arms to reach down toward Bernard, who swoons in his white cowl in Christ's arms. Bernard's head seems to rest on the Crucified's right arm, bringing to mind the verse "His right hand embraces me" (Song 8:3).

Sr. Suzanne Mattiuzzo, when she was at Our Lady of the Mississippi Abbey, copied the Ribalta *amplexus*, replacing Saint

---

[21] *Exordium magnum cisterciense*, ed. Bruno Griesser (Rome: Editiones Cistercienses, 1961), 2.7. The translation is mine.

Bernard with a Cistercian nun. The nun in her white cowl and black veil occupies the privileged place for the embrace. Theologically we might call this "substitutionary imitation": as Bernard strove to imitate Christ, so Cistercians generations later strive to imitate Bernard and envision themselves obtaining the same mutual love of Christ that Bernard obtained. Gender certainly does not matter in the soul's passion for union with the body of the Crucified.

Abraham van Diepenbeek, ca.1630, painted the embrace of Saint Lütgard. Her hagiographer takes pains to recount a story parallel to the *amplexus Bernardi*:

> She hurried to church. . . . At the entrance of the church, Christ, bloody and affixed to the cross, appeared to her: and detaching his arm from the cross, embraced her, and brought her mouth to the wound in his right side, whence she drew such sweetness that always afterwards she was more vigorous and eager in the service of God.[22]

Though van Diepenbeek's Christ is unbloody, he faithfully depicts Christ detaching only his right arm to embrace Saint Lütgard. Christ gazes down at the top of Lütgard's head, while she, in her Cistercian white cowl and black veil, gazes not at Christ but at the wound in his side. Lütgard's arms are crossed at the wrists in front of her breast, where one puts one's arms before prostration. The painting thus implies another parallel with the prostrate Bernard. Lütgard's gaze recalls Song 4:9: "You have wounded my heart, my sister, my bride, with a single glance of your eye." Perhaps she also contemplates the wound in Christ's side in preparation for bringing her mouth there and drawing forth sweet strength.

Jeffrey Hamburger brings to light a wonderful handheld (118 x 84 mm) devotional book from Flanders or the Rhineland

---

[22] AASS Junii 4:1.13.193.

at the turn of the fourteenth century.[23] A miniature covering a two-page spread in the Song of Songs series depicts a dramatic encounter between Christ and the *sponsa*. At the top left, Christ and the *sponsa* are pictured in a mutual embrace, then entering the garden. At the bottom left, the *sponsa* sits on a low bench, holding in her right hand a spear that points directly across the center-page margin to the wound in Christ's side. The *sponsa*'s left hand seems to be brushing her veil back from her eye, as if illustrating that same passage from Song 4:9: "You have wounded my heart, my sister, my bride, with a single glance of your eye." Her glance, as well as the spear, penetrates.

On the right-hand page, the resurrected Christ appears full length and completely naked, which is rare in medieval art. Some of the *arma Christi* make an appearance: the cross, the column of flagellation, the scourge, rope, nails, and crown of thorns. The buds on the cross indicate that it is the *arbor vitae*, the tree of life. Christ is only loosely nailed through the feet, his left foot to the column, his right stepping across his body to the cross. His left hand holds two nails; his right arm wraps around the column, holding the scourge and pointing to his own side wound in a typical *ostentatio vulneris* gesture. The side wound is the entrance, as in Rev 3:20: "Behold, I stand at the door and knock; if you open the door, I will come in to you and eat with you, and you with me." Hamburger comments on the Saint Walburg drawings, but his thought could apply equally well to this extraordinary miniature in *The Rothschild Canticles*: "Employing the rhetoric of wounding sight, the drawings enact the *imitatio Christi* according to the script spelled out in the Song of Songs. The Canticle provides the cues for a passion consummated in the nun's body as well as Christ's, with the heart of each being the place where this ecstatic introspection in enacted." In addition, the *sponsa* takes

---

[23] Jeffrey F. Hamburger, *The Rothschild Canticles: Art and Mysticism in Flanders and the Rhineland Circa 1300* (New Haven and London: Yale University Press, 1990), 72–77.

on the traditionally masculine role, holding the phallic spear, while Christ appears in a traditionally feminine role, naked, vulnerable, and penetrated.

A book of poems and line drawings by Christophe Lebreton, who was one of the Cistercian martyrs of the Atlas monastery, was published posthumously. On page 162, facing the final chapter, titled "Jusqu'a l'extrême—L'accomplissement du don" ("All the way to the end—the accomplishment of the gift"), is a simple drawing of a cross with all four beams open-ended, with a vertical wound. In the lower left quadrant, there is a sketch of an eye, eyebrow, and nose, and slightly parted lips. The eye's shape is a horizontal mandorla; the opening of the lips is akin to the wound on the cross.[24] Perhaps Fr. Lebreton was himself thinking of that same passage from Song 4:9: "You have wounded my heart, my sister, my bride, with a single one of your eyes."

In Sermons 3 and 4 on the Song of Songs Bernard explains the kiss of the Lord's feet, hands, and mouth. He says that the soul makes progress in kissing the Lord: the penitent or newly converted kisses the feet, the seeker or one making progress kisses the hand, and the lover or more perfect kisses the mouth.[25] Guerric's sermons and the medieval art examined here offer a similar progression in contemplation. The kiss of the feet is *imitatio*; the kiss of the hand is contemplation; the kiss of the mouth is union. One who has received this mystical kiss seeks again that intimate experience: "the one who drinks still thirsts for more" (Sir 24:21).

Nikos Kazantzakis wrote of Saint Francis that he was praying on this Feast of the Triumph of the Cross when suddenly angels brought his devotion to fulfillment. Saint Francis stands

---

[24] Christophe Lebreton, *Born from the Gaze of God*, MW 137 (Collegeville, MN: Cistercian Publications, 2013), 162.

[25] Bernard, SC 4.1; Bernard of Clairvaux, *Sermons on the Song of Songs*, vol. 1, trans Kilian Walsh, CF 4 (Kalamazoo, MI: Cistercian Publications, 1976), 21.

crucified in the air, with rays of light streaming from Christ's wounds to Francis's own hands, feet, and side, and Francis receives the stigmata. His imitation of the Crucified becomes visible marks in his own flesh, as the wounds become the signs of the victory on the cross. Even the resurrected Christ still bears his wounds, so he can offer them to Thomas to examine them with his fingers.[26]

Our brothers at Munkeby have invited us to make our personal retreat at their monastery. One of the first to take them up on their offer was Sr. Hanne-Maria, who biked the sixty kilometers north. She loves to hike in the natural beauty of the countryside, and as part of her retreat she followed the pilgrim trail that winds around Munkeby Mariakloster and the ruins from the thirteenth century. She discovered that parts of the trail were well-marked, other parts not. Some places were overgrown, and it was not clear where the path continued. The pilgrim trail to Nidaros Cathedral has a particular symbol, a red cross, and the trail is marked with posts bearing this symbol. Sr. Hanne-Maria, when she could not discern by looking at the trail where she should go next, began looking for the next post bearing the pilgrim symbol. *Ah! It's THERE I want to go.* She realized she was looking for the next cross, and this became a parable for her retreat.

This is the way it is in our lives, if we understand the mystery of the cross. Something that seems bad, and often feels really terrible, becomes something good, something redemptive, something that brings new life. To go further on our earthly pilgrimage, to come closer to God's heart, we need to keep looking for the next cross, the next challenge, the next difficulty—which will cause us to grow, and bear good fruit in the end. Crosses are already there, posted on our path. We need to keep seeking the cross, the sign of our salvation, the place where Jesus is most like us, and we like him.

---

[26] Nikos Kazantzakis, *Saint Francis*, trans. P. A. Bien (New York: Simon and Schuster, 1962), 316–18.

The pilgrim symbol, by the way, is a deep red, the color of blood, the color of ripe plums.

Plums

Sr. Maria Rafael Bartlett, OCSO

On a gray, humid morning in August,
I picked plums
from a rich crop in our small
monastery orchard. I climbed the narrow
metal ladder, up into the canopy of leaves
with its fruit like round planets
suspended in the green.

Having filled one tub, I looked; I studied
the plumness of a single plum: the taut,
smooth, rubbery skin; how its cloudy bruised blue,
under the warm pressure of my fingers
stained to a blush;
the crystallized, honeyed droplet of juice
where the thin skin split;
the shallow cleft curving across the
cool orb of the fruit; the sweet
dense flesh.

With what relish
are we all
taken and consumed
by the holy mouth of God,
and with what tender delicacy
does he remove
from the center of each,
the hard,
unyielding stone.

October

Ordinary Joy

Sr. Maria Rafael Bartlett, OCSO

It reveals a great deal about Norway, and about Tautra, that in writing about three different months, I find myself describing each month as beautiful. When you live your life deeply, planted in one stable place, as we are here in our island monastery, you learn to receive the seasonal changes in a uniquely rich way. This chapter sings of October, a month that gathers up the sharp chill and the vivid colors of autumn while carrying in its arms the scents and lingering mellow warmth of late summer.

Like all seasons in a monastery, months are deeply associated with the worship of the liturgical year. October is in a way an "ordinary" month, not associated with any solemnities or major Cistercian feast days. It is not barren of liturgical memorials, but it lacks the abundance of feasts that some months are laden with. In October we celebrate Saint Francis of Assisi, Saint Teresa of Avila, Saint Thérèse of Lisieux, and Saint Luke. Such a month can be said to reflect the "ordinary joy" of our life of faith, a joy not centered so much in festive celebration but in the simplicity and strength of a living faith, renewed day by day. In another sense, in the Christian life there is no such thing as an ordinary day. Boredom and a kind of heedlessness happen to us when we are disconnected within from the saving truth of our faith, from the imperishable mercy revealed in the paschal mystery.

Because so much of monastic life is repetition, the days have an outward sameness. It takes a degree of intense inward aliveness, traditionally called "being recollected," if we are to keep the fire of our love from dwindling to cold ashes. This is where our monastic practices such as *lectio divina*, silent prayer, and an engaged participation in liturgy come into their own as sources of nourishment for the heart. Without them, we starve, and our energy diminishes. We cease to be fully alive in our monastic vocation.

The Eucharist is a unique gift from God, giving us the real and whole presence of Jesus to be assimilated by both body and soul. Yet when I am distracted and forget the *reality* we are celebrating, I find myself bored, and the too-familiar ritual and words seem empty of meaning. Our practice of a deeply interior silence through our days is intended to amplify and integrate for us the resonant meanings of all the activities in the monastic horarium. It requires a vigorous effort and commitment from us. It is not a silence for its own sake, but, set alight by the Word of Scripture and prayer, it is an inner space of encounter, of receiving and responding to the presence of God. We begin afresh each day. I have heard a nun of over ninety announce, "*Now* I feel I'm beginning."

Autumn and early winter here bring a light with its own distinctive quality. The radiance of the daylight on days of sunshine is often made more striking in contrast with cool temperatures, leafless trees, and earlier nights. In every season, we can be open to perceiving nature's rich language expressing something of the One who created it, and created *us* able to see and hear.

"Day unto day pours forth . . ."

The autumn light blesses
like fire; trees and grass
are soaked in golden flame.
Yellow leaves are prayer flags
against a sky Tibetan blue.
In a wind drenched

with the sound of the sea, the leaves in the treetops
shake like bells.

What does the sky's blue
speak? It breathes; cries out
unceasingly.

What sings
this October wind, moving
the woods to joy?

What word
has this radiant harvest moon for us,
near dawn?

Listen:
let the vocabulary of creation
ignite the word
inside.

October is something of a transition, a bridge between the
sparkle and abundance of late summer and the austerity of
winter's bare trees and the terse hours of daylight. We prepare
ourselves inwardly for winter's new relationship to night. For
me, this has spiritual consequences: a deepening of interiority
as autumn moves towards winter. The inside of the monastery
takes up this new emphasis: candles are lit in the refectory at
dawn and dusk, and when it gets cold, we light a comforting
fire in the wood burner after Vigils.

Writing about autumn brings to my mind the spiritual associations night and darkness hold for me. I am always touched
by the psalm phrase, "If I say, 'Surely the darkness shall cover
me, and the light around me become night,' even the darkness
is not dark to you, and the night is as clear as the day" (Ps
139:11-12). This is the psalm that begins, "O Lord, you have

searched me and known me" (Ps 139:1). Our being so intimately known to God who loved us into creation is both a joy and a fear. His seeing my sins more clearly than I do, seeing through every self-justification and falsehood, frightens me at times. I sometimes feel scared of my transparency to his gaze. I can feel afraid to lose his love. Yet he assures me he understands my fears. His acceptance cauterizes the dark wound of my resistance. As he forgives us, he proves that for his tremendous love, even our blackest "night is clear as the day": seen as it is, then cleansed so it lets in light.

When I pray in silence before the Blessed Sacrament in the early morning after Vigils, my inner experience is most often one of desert aridity and darkness, what feels like absence. It is faith, and the love that underpins faith, that enlightens the night with a Presence I know is with me always. Faith has to grow strong enough to remain awake in the night.

A saint very dear to me whose feast day is on the first of October (only a memorial in the Cistercian Order, but surely a solemnity in heaven) is Saint Thérèse of Lisieux, the nineteenth-century French Carmelite. Thérèse practiced a heroic faith in very ordinary circumstances, seeking and finding God in every small detail of her religious life, in spite of considerable personal suffering. Her Little Way reveals a surprisingly mature, radical spirituality, yet she had no mystical experiences. She fell asleep in prayer regularly. She confirmed that she had never heard the voice of Jesus, but she was absolutely certain of his indwelling presence. In her final excruciating illness, in which she felt God was utterly absent and she doubted his existence, she clung to her love for God by pure and steely faith. ("I sing what I want to believe.") For me, that is another form of the psalmist's experience in asserting "night is as clear as the day." For Thérèse, the darkness of her physical and spiritual suffering was made transparent to God by the sheer force of her love. His love still entered in, feeding her determined faith.

In fine weather, summer on Tautra has a shining beauty that constantly compels our gaze: boats glide by on the fjord, birds fly past the refectory windows, or sometimes just their shadows move past as they fly high near the roof. There is a satiny shimmer on the water from late afternoon that beckons like a golden path. The endlessly shifting color, texture, and movement of the fjord waters beside our monastery speak to me of the delicate impermanence of the present moment, and they speak too of eternity.

Eternity is an everlasting "now," beyond our imagining. There is an intimate bond between the precious present moment continually dissolving into the next, with the mysterious timelessness of eternity. We can never grasp either. We can only choose to try to anchor ourselves in an immersion in the now as into a moving stream heading for the distant, open sea. That immersion, when it happens, is a mindful vigilance that somehow engages our whole being. We experience all of life as transitory, yet in the life of faith, our very transitoriness is inhabited by the holy, by the living and holy One. Thus there is a merger in our monastic life between the present moment and eternal life.

Another feature of autumn that brings to mind images of eternity is the beginning of the vivid sunsets of early winter. If we walk along the narrow road from the monastery to the point at which the houses end, we face in the distance a long view of the fjord as it blurs into softly layered hills. This is where we see the sun setting, and the tender beauty of the day's end is a profound utterance from the landscape. Soft pastel rose- or peach-colored light spreads over the painted wooden houses and the murmuring fjord before disappearing behind pale, watercolor hills. Like the approach of dawn, the transfiguration of day into night is a powerful encounter with the forces of nature.

The island becomes quieter with the coming of autumn. In summer, we have many visitors to the island as well as guests staying at the monastery, and our small shop is often bustling with customers. The bird life that is an essential part of Tautra life as a national bird reserve means that summertime is noisy with the raucous calls and screams of seagulls, which hatch their young on our stony shore. The range of sounds produced by gulls is striking, and it is *not* a melodious sound. For me, autumn brings the relief of their departure for the winter.

We are lucky to usually have several volunteers during our busy summer season, but often we have fewer during autumn. We close our shop or reduce its hours once the island is once more emptier, and the heightened summer activity begins to recede. Those of us who swim throughout the summer, although we are robust enough to brave the cold water, cannot sustain the icy temperatures of the fjord beyond the beginning of October. We proudly call ourselves Vikings, but we have our limits!

What does it mean to give oneself to what we call ordinary life, when there are no special events or celebrations? Nuns are as subject as anyone to distractions and wandering thoughts, and the more full the days are with special events, the harder it is simply to be in the present moment, in silent prayer and in the liturgy, for example. An ordinary day has a calm spaciousness about it that invites focus on seeking God in each part of the day as it unfolds: from the silent prayerfulness of early morning after Vigils and adoration, to Lauds, Mass, Terce, and chapter, then in our daily work, at meals, at meridian rest, and so on as the day flows in its smooth monastic rhythm. When a monk or nun is truly mature in the spiritual life, inward spaciousness can be found in the midst of hectic activity, but for me as one still in formation, that isn't yet the case. I need my ordinary days.

In our monastery, all the cells have a view of the fjord. My cell is on the ground floor, and I hope I will always cherish the privilege of living so close to water. While there is a special holiday quality to going to bed to the sound of gulls and the whoosh of water on the shore, I find it difficult to sleep with the glow of evening daylight pushing against my curtains. I have to induce darkness artificially with a black eye cover. I rejoice when evening begins to bring darkness, promoting a more natural sleep. It feels symbolic to me about the place of darkness in our lives, that even in the loveliest Norwegian summer, something is missing. We see no stars in summer. I relish the first day of autumn in which I see stars again, before Vigils or in the evening. I wonder if heaven, eternal life in God, will have both darkness and light.

For Norwegians, especially those who live with the seasonal extremes of the far north, the dense, barely relieved darkness of winter means that the summer light is to be celebrated and savored in a specially intense way. There are places in which, when light returns, people stay up all night to rejoice with friends in the gift of light and warmth, to celebrate being released from the tight boundaries of long darkness. That seems a kind of Easter experience.

Although it is days of sunlight that come most readily to mind as I write, we do have rain and dismal days. The entire region of Trøndelag with its nearness to the coast is one of unsettled, changeable weather. On an island this can be particularly true: "four seasons in a single day" is the saying. September and October are generally the wettest months.

October can be a wet month with high winds and driving rain. The fjord in a storm appears dramatically transformed from a gently moving body of tidal water, sometimes as still as a calm lake, into what one sister described as a beast. The water then looks gun-metal grey and churns violently, waves beating against the shore and whitecaps racing across the water. The sky on these days is forbidding, with smoky clouds lowering themselves down over the land and water.

When a severe storm comes to the island, it can be a spectacular show of force. The Norwegian meteorological service is uncannily accurate in predicting storms, almost down to the minute. Gale force winds batter the monastery, and the wind in the trees has a rushing sound like the sea. Our trees bend and sometimes break, but the most alarming sight is the buckling of our huge walls of glass. These windows in the church, cloister, and refectory can be seen to quiver under the pressure of powerful winds, but in fact they are designed to bend. When

I first witnessed this, I didn't trust the safety of the glass and was unnerved as a storm boomed against the house during Compline one dark evening. I felt unsafe in bed that night and lay listening uneasily to the noise and sensation of attack on the fabric of the monastery. In the morning, all was intact and the storm had subsided. The next time such weather came, I was prepared to trust a little—and it became easier each time. Now I rely on the sturdiness and clever design of the building, which was created precisely to withstand the fierce weather that can assail a Norwegian island.

It impresses me that God has created us to use our faith to bolster ourselves against the turbulence of misfortune and suffering, so that we too can bend rather than be shattered into pieces. For me, the personal equivalent of the bending glass is the ready acknowledgement of pain and distress: I am not to maintain a rigid front but to *let* anguish move me, bend me—to truly feel that pain is what leads me to know my utter need for God's help, and so I pray that he will be my strength in tempestuous times.

A particular beauty in autumn is the color of the leaves. Behind our monastery, which is built with overlapping squares of slate in autumnal colors (gold, rust, brown, . . .), is a narrow strip of mossy, unruly grass and then a line of aspen trees. These are a screen between our home and the fjord when they are in full leaf. In autumn, the pretty, rounded leaves turn a vibrant yellow. Against the backdrop of a blue fjord in sunshine, the stand of trees is a beautiful sight. Sometimes a golden light rests just on the tops of the line of trees. Aspen leaves are spoken of as having leaves that quake or shiver; they are continually in movement, touched by even the faintest of breezes. I imagine a soft sound, like a melody made by small bells, when I see this trembling of the leaves. I don't think the word *quaking* fits the movement of the leaves, though I've read it in botanical information about aspens. The movement is too joyful for that. They *quiver* with delight.

I find the autumn aspen leaves so lovely that I am often mesmerized by the beauty of a single smooth fallen leaf, unquenchable yellow on our dense green grass. I take countless photographs of the bright trees standing in an iconic line, but even the successful shots don't encounter the beauty the way the eye does, are not pierced to the heart by it. It always strikes me as wonderful that the end represented by falling leaves happens when many of them are at their most brilliant, aflame with colors—deep red, copper, gold, yellow. I want to burn like that when my time comes to let go of the tree, and let myself fall.

As we live on an island, the landscape we appreciate each day is very much dominated by the fjord but also by the sky. Friends of mine from England who have visited me here often remark on the wonder of the changing skies. Whether glimpsed between city skyscrapers or from a car window, the sky is lovely everywhere, but on a low-lying island the canvas of the sky seems immense, and nothing competes with it visually. We become conscious of its features in a fresh way. The shifting textures of clouds, piled in soft pillowy shapes or like brush-strokes of wispy white against the blue, tinged with the tones of dawn or sunset, or ominous and heavy-laden with rain— these continually changing skies mean that I turn my head towards the sky over and over each day. I walk, I turn back, turn back again, watching the sky. Has it changed from the marvel I just observed? Does it look different from the end of the road? I hear myself exclaim, "Oh! I've never seen it so beautiful!"

I love to photograph the very tops of trees with ribbons of blown cloud just above the branches, looking as if a wind has just combed through the white. It conveys a sense of time passing swiftly, in silence. As the winter draws nearer, sometimes in early evening a luminous round moon is suspended, huge and solitary, low in the darkening sky by our guesthouses. I stop in my tracks and gaze at it. It takes all speech away. There's no articulating my thoughts at these moments of contact with beauty: it is a silent inward encounter with mystery.

When I was in my rebellious teenage years, I remember questioning the description of nature as "beautiful," asserting scornfully that to call anything beautiful was merely a subjective label with no actual reality or essence that warranted this description: "We call the sea beautiful because we've heard people say that." I clearly had not discovered the encounter with mystery, an experience that is profoundly personal but responsive to a quality of loveliness inherent in the natural world. And now, to make up for my unfeeling youth, I am surrounded on every side by an overflow of beauty.

Another element in our life in which I see beauty is the group of sisters with whom I live. Before each Office in church, some of us like to stand briefly as a way of preparing ourselves to pray with attention, and when I am standing, often I find myself observing the ordinary loveliness of my sisters. The vulnerability of a face at rest, a face with eyes closed in prayer, the distinctiveness of each person's hands and how she holds them, relaxed in her lap or tensely clasped together, conveying a tension she is bearing; how our skin looks at different ages, the uniqueness of each person, how the veil and habit hang differently on each of us, the sweet (and on a bad day, bitter) familiarity of each sister. This is my family and my home, and that is beautiful and to be cherished in itself.

We slowly learn God's endless creativity when it comes to presenting us with ways in which to grow. Struggling with the vagaries of relationships and what our relating tells us about ourselves is a key form of personal maturing in the monastic life. When there is conflict, I can think indignantly, "I didn't come here for this!"—but in that, I am wrong. And as someone has said, if we lived with a group of saints, what challenge would there be for us?

In the Cistercian day, we spend many hours in choir, praising God and praying for the world and ourselves. The sung liturgy is the form of prayer we spend most time with. It has often been observed that choir is a reflection of what is going on within community, and it is also a place of continual work to relinquish the power of the ego. If I'm praying in silence in church or my cell, I could occasionally entertain the idea of myself as impressively holy. When I enter my place in choir and the Office begins, I am face to face with the truth: I see myself irritated by my neighbor's sighing and throat-clearing (even if I do the same), annoyed and judgmental about how sister so-and-so is singing too loudly and off-pitch (compared of course to my own melodic perfection); I am distracted from attentiveness by the other side of choir singing too rapidly; I am consumed with thoughts of how we could improve choir. It is a hotbed of prayerful peace interrupted by the ceaseless clamorings of self-will. That ordinary inner battle as we squarely regard our own self-centeredness and try to transcend it is a significant part of our life.

Because we sing our liturgy in Norwegian, for me it is a double struggle. The words' not being in my own mother tongue means they don't engage my attention as easily as English would. It is even easier for me to be distracted. But the other side of the choir experience is that singing helps to lift the heart to God. As Saint Augustine famously said, "The one who sings, prays twice." Singing gives us a pathway to forgetting ourselves in praise. For me, once I have navigated the straits of overreaction to others, and admitted that I don't sound so wonderful myself, I can usually set aside those acknowledged feelings and find my way to focus on the Lord through the joy of song. The choir itself involves an imperfect unity among us that reflects the Christian life. Perceived in that way, being in a monastic choir is in fact a little miracle: a unity not created by us. It is a gift from God.

During the seasons of abundance and harvest, we try to grow as much of our own food as we can, and there is a marvelous variety of flowers in summer for placing before the altar, in guest bedrooms as a welcome, and in our refectory on our feast day. Our chaplain, Father Anthony, who is an Irish Cistercian monk but has lived in Norway for many years now, grows spectacular lettuce of different varieties in his unusual shore-side garden. These lettuces are blessed by the moist salt air from the fjord, by Anthony's steadfast labor, and by a soil enriched with the tang of seaweed. We enjoy this produce until well into October. His lettuce is pretty, too, large, and some with curly scalloped edges, others with a pale purple tinge, all of it fresh, crisp, and health-giving.

Another treasure of the autumn months is wild mushrooms. Our Norwegian sister, Hanne-Maria, was for some time the only source of expertise in finding and identifying safe edible wild mushrooms. Now our Polish sister, Renata, who is in First Vows, is equally passionate about searching for these woodland specialties. The first time she was given permission to go and find some, she was as thrilled as a child on Christmas morning. To eat these mushrooms, which smell so enticing when fried in butter, you have to trust absolutely the sisters who collect them. The first time Renata had brought some back from the woods, I was briefly hesitant at dinner time, but no longer. She says, "I go into the forest, and it's as if they're all there for me!" There seems no competition to gather mushrooms on Tautra. For Renata, and perhaps for some others, the forest is a magical, favorite place on the island. Near our monastery, where I've described the houses as coming to an end, there begins another part of the island, where cows are often pastured and there is woodland. It feels a delightfully hidden world inside the shadowy forest, with sounds of the fjord's waves muted and birdsong magnified. When I enter there, I look up—at the patterns made by treetops against the sky—not at the edible treasures under my feet.

At about the midpoint of the island there is also a plain wooden structure that rises up above the trees, a birdwatching tower. As you follow a marked-off path through woods from the road to the tower, occasionally you see some of the dark brown ponies that live on Tautra, big liquid eyes just visible through a thick rough mane. Just near the tower, there is a lagoon that is part of a large farm opposite our monastery. This wetland is wild and beautiful: large birds flap up from the water or circle overhead; the pond is edged with long green grasses and is set in a broad space with woodland on one side, the silvery fjord on the other. It always teems with birdlife, but without the screaming gulls. I have a special love for this wetland. This year, in winter, our sister Christina, who is Dutch and an expert skater, created a circular ice rink just beyond the lagoon, closer to the big white farmhouse. We have a knack of savoring all our seasons.

For me, October is a time for gradually drawing back from the bright shine of the island summer, from the interaction of visits from friends, from the pleasure of swimming in the fjord and sitting outside in the sunshine. I am grateful for the changing seasons, and I welcome autumn as it carries me gently towards another enfolding winter. I put new batteries in my camera and set my gaze on the sky, the trees, the water. Tautra is beautiful every day.

Lights in the Darkness

Sr. Anne Elizabeth Sweet, OCSO

I will give you treasures of darkness. (Isa 45:3)

Here in Norway, one really feels the darkness during the month of November. Daylight Saving Time has ended. It is still dark around 8 a.m. on All Saints Day, and light dawns progressively later as the month progresses. I remember my first Christmas here: the sun rose around 10:30 a.m. and set around 1:30 p.m. In early November, the evening darkness begins around 4:30 p.m. Each year, the experience of so much darkness still comes as a bit of a shock to my system.

Norwegians have several practical helps that enable them to see the way through this physical darkness. Reflective poles line the side of the road so that drivers do not veer off. Pedestrians wear reflective clothing so as to be easily seen in traffic. Bicycles, baby carriages, and dogs are similarly marked. Safety is a high priority. Candles and lamps adorn the windows of every home like beacons piercing the darkness. With the coming of Advent, the traditional candelabra shine brightly, pointing to him who is the true light and whose coming into the world we will soon celebrate. In the midst of so much darkness, life beckons, life goes on.

Already in my first "dark season" here, I discovered "treasures of darkness" (Isa 45:3). First, there were the stars. I had arrived here in mid-May 2006, well into the season of light—almost total daylight for twenty-four hours. So it was thrilling, when the darkness did come, to see the stars. And I saw them as if for the first time with the delight of a child.

"Stars!!!!!!!!!!!!!!!! Look!!!!!!!!!!" I am reminded of God's word to Abraham: "Look toward heaven and count the stars, if you are able . . ." (Gen 15:5). And of course, I couldn't. It was impossible against the backdrop of the wide expanse of sky that is ours on Tautra. There were countless stars! The stars: treasured gifts in the darkness from the hand of the Creator. "He determines the number of the stars; he gives to all of them their names" (Ps 147:4). Gazing toward the night sky, one feels one's own littleness and insignificance. Nevertheless, just as the Creator gives a name to each star, so he does to each of us. We are not insignificant in his eyes; we matter, we are called by name. "The stars shone in their watches, and were glad; he called them, and they said, 'Here we are!' They shone with gladness for him who made them" (Bar 3:34).

Might Baruch's words be a reminder of what we are really supposed to be about: answering the call of our Creator, shining with gladness not only for him, but for the world—our everyday world? "Let your light shine before others, so that they may see your good works and give glory to your Father in heaven" (Matt 5:16).

The prophet Daniel directs our attention to yet another significance of the stars. Daniel's angelic guide assures him that in the age to come, those who are wise and righteous "shall shine like the brightness of the sky, . . . like the stars for ever and ever" (Dan 12:3). If this is the destiny of the wise and righteous, *now* is the time for us to so live as to be among them.

> *The heavens are telling the glory of God. . . . night to night declares knowledge.* (Ps 19:1-2)

Perhaps the most thrilling treasure of Norway's dark months is the spectacular display of Northern Lights, which are visible on clear nights. In mid-Norway, the lights are most often a bright Kelly green in color. Sometimes they appear as pale-green-tinted clouds. How does one know that they are Northern Lights and not clouds? Sister Hanne-Maria, our native

Norwegian, explained, "it's quite simple; you can see the stars through them."

Such was the case last night, a November night. I had to go over to the guesthouse after Vespers. As I came around the corner of the church, I saw a large arc of light in the sky, the shape of a rainbow. Its hue had a hint of pale, pale green. "Is that Northern Lights?" asked a young American volunteer from California. "Yes," I said. She became so excited. "Wait until she sees them in action," I thought. "I can barely see them," she said. "Keep watching, they change," I answered.

Leaving her standing on the path, I continued on my way, my eyes glued to the sky. When I went into the guesthouse, I was met by a young woman from Hungary who was here to discern a vocation to monastic life. "I saw the Northern Lights!" she excitedly exclaimed. "Keep watching," I said, "they will change."

Back at the monastery shortly before Compline, I noticed a group of sisters gathered in the dark cloister, looking out the large window. As soon as someone sees Northern Lights, the word spreads fast, and the sisters are quickly at the windows or even outside, as they are best viewed unhampered by any artificial light. The Northern Lights had begun to do their thing as the arc was waxing and waning: rays of light streaming across the sky in every direction. "Ohhhhhhhh" "Aaaaaahhh-hhhhhhhh." There we were, grown women squealing with the delight of children, running around, gazing in every direction, not wanting to miss a thing. And perhaps that is as it should be: "Unless you become like children you will never enter the kingdom of heaven" (Matt 18:3).

Whenever I wake up during these dark nights, I immediately get up and look out the window. Can I see Northern Lights? Once, as I lay in bed and watched, it seemed that God was waving ribbons of light across the northern sky. For me, the experience is always a gift, a touch of beauty sent to me personally by the Lord.

"When I look at your heavens, the work of your fingers . . . what are human beings that you are mindful of them, mortals, that you care for them?" (Ps 8:3-4). And yet God does care, ever so much, for each and every one of us, calling us by name, loving us with an everlasting love. So wonderful is this knowledge!

All Saints Day: November 1

The path of the righteous is like the light of dawn, which shines brighter and brighter until full day. (Prov 4:18)

"A saint is someone whom the light shines through," I once heard a priest say during a children's liturgy as he pointed to the stained glass windows. This was some forty years ago, in a little country church in southwest Iowa, and I've never forgotten it. And indeed, the windows do come to life when the sun shines through them—then and only then—as they are not visible in the darkness. These figures are recognized as saints because when they were alive, they lived in such a manner that the divine light shone through them. They lived in imitation of Jesus: people of prayer and good works, people willing to share in the suffering of Christ so that they might one day share in his glory (Phil 3:10-11). They were truly lights in the darkness in their own day, and so they remain for us today.

It is interesting to note that Saint Paul, in his letters, speaks of all believers as "saints" or "holy ones"—while they are still alive! See, for example, 1 Corinthians 1:2 and 2 Corinthians 1:1. In fact, if one looks at the opening verses of his letters, one finds this address in almost all of them. Believers are addressed as such not by virtue of what *they* have done but rather because of what Christ has done for them in baptism, bringing them to life in his own divine life. Thus the task of the Christian is to be continually transformed in his image. As Paul writes to the Corinthians in his second letter, "For it is the God who said, 'Let light shine out of darkness,' who has shone in our hearts to give the light of the knowledge of the glory of God in the face of Jesus Christ" (2 Cor 4:6). It is a treasure we hold in the "clay jars," the human vessels that we are, "so that it may be made clear that this extraordinary power belongs to God and does not come from us" (2 Cor 4:7).

In a similar vein, Saint Benedict exhorts us in his Rule, the rule by which we live, to open our eyes to the "deifying light" that comes from God (Prol. 9).[1] So the Latin text literally reads, a point that is unfortunately missed in many translations. The "deifying light" makes us more and more like Christ, the true Light, in whose image we are made.

So we are indeed among the saints and holy ones, striving to live as saints and holy ones in the footsteps of Jesus. And isn't that what the church has always taught us when speaking of the communion of saints: those on earth as well as those in heaven?

"All Saints Day" is also commemorated in the Lutheran or state Church here in Norway, but here it is a day of commemoration of all those who have died in the past year. Roman Catholics commemorate the dead on November 2, All Souls Day. The first time I saw "All Saints Day" as the theme of the Sunday liturgy in our local Lutheran parish, I was really surprised, for a question I am frequently asked by non-Catholic retreatants and visitors to our monastery is "why do Catholics pray to the saints?" It was only as I learned more about what Norwegian Lutherans believe about life after death that the question made sense to me.

All Souls Day: November 2

The souls of the righteous are in the hand of God. In the time of their visitation they shall shine forth. (Wis 3:1, 7)

The Norwegians have the custom of putting lighted candles on the graves of loved ones during the month of November.

---

[1] Leonard J. Doyle, trans., *The Rule of Saint Benedict* (Collegeville, MN: Liturgical Press, 1948), 2001. RB verse references are cited from RB 1980, ed. and trans. Timothy Fry (Collegeville, MN: Liturgical Press, 1981).

I was so touched when I first saw it, as I immediately thought of our Christian belief in the everlasting light and life in which our departed loved ones now share. What a beautiful practice and reminder, I thought. However, in conversation with a woman retreatant, I soon discovered that this was not the association that the Norwegians were making. In fact, they were not aware of any special reason for putting candles on the graves. "Why then do you do it?" I asked. Her answer was most surprising, "I don't know. We just do it."

As my conversation with our retreatant continued, I learned that most Norwegians do not believe that our departed loved ones share in the eternal light and life of Christ immediately after death, but rather, this is something for which they wait on the last day when all mortal bodies are raised from the dead. Until that time, those who have died are asleep in the dust of the earth.

This belief is very evident in the funeral liturgy of the Norwegian Lutheran Church. I attended my first Norwegian funeral almost eleven years after I came to Norway. One of our elderly neighbors who had been a good friend of the monastery was buried from our church. The emphasis was very much on saying farewell to the departed, expressed both in the memories recounted by family and friends and the attention given to reading the messages on the floral arrangements that surrounded the casket. In fact, these took up the greater part of the service. There were some short Scripture readings, all pertaining to resurrection, and a homily by the presiding priest, but no mention of the life that the departed experiences immediately after death. My experience was the same some months later when we had another neighbor's funeral in our church.

Recently I spoke with a Norwegian Lutheran priest about my experiences, and he confirmed my impressions. Indeed, it is their belief that after death, we lie asleep until the final resurrection of the dead.

Both my conversation with our retreatant and the priest's comments—as well as my experience of the funeral liturgies—

were jarring. I could not imagine *not* believing that our loved ones continued in existence after death and that they were even more alive now in eternal life. When my own mother died, the prayer card distributed by the mortuary read, "entered into life: November 3, 1924; entered into the fullness of life: March 26, 2008." Not only were these words comforting; I have had personal experience of the truth of their reality. It has happened several times that I suddenly became aware of my mother's presence and love still very much with me, and on one occasion quite unexpectedly, I even heard her speaking to me with words that she often used when she was alive. I've had the same experience with other deceased friends and relatives with whom I was close.

Before coming to the awareness of what most Norwegian Lutherans believed—or rather didn't believe—regarding death and life continuing after death, I had written on several occasions to friends of the community who had lost a parent or loved one: "I pray that you will experience their love for you and their presence with you even beyond death." I didn't realize, of course, that these words would be meaningless to them. Nevertheless, it happened on one occasion that someone said in reply, "You know, now that you say that, I did have an experience like that one time after my father died." He went on to share how that experience came about—very unexpectedly—and how much that had meant to him.

Reflecting on these experiences, it occurred to me that perhaps our monastic presence here in Norway, our sharing of our faith and our personal experiences with retreatants and guests, can be a light illumining the experiences that others carry within them.

Dedication of Churches: November 9 and 19

In your light, we see light. (Ps 36:9)

Twice during November we celebrate feasts of the Dedication of a Church: on November 9, the Lateran Basilica in Rome, the parish church of the Holy Father, and the dedication of our own diocesan cathedral on November 19. The latter is a new feast for us, as St. Olav's Church in Trondheim was dedicated only in 2016. All of us went to Trondheim to participate in this grand event. Among the highlights of the ceremony for me were the anointing of the altar with chrism and the lighting of the five incense holders on the altar, and the anointing of the walls of the church and the lighting of the consecration candles around the church. This holy anointing symbolizes that the church has been solemnly blessed and dedicated to God. The consecration candles mark the spot where the walls, or in the case of St. Olav's in Trondheim, the pillars, were anointed. Each year, on the anniversary of the dedication of the church, the consecration candles are lighted as they are here at Tautra on May 12, the anniversary of the dedication of our own church.

As we all are well aware, the church is much more than a building. In fact, if it weren't for the people who are the church, the building would be meaningless. After all, Jesus' words to Peter had nothing to do with a building: "you are Peter and on this rock I will build my church" (Matt 16:18). This emphasis on the people as the church is confirmed throughout the New Testament, where the Greek word *ekklēsía* occurs (for example, Rom 16:5; 1 Cor 12:28; Rev 3:22). Our Cistercian constitutions remind us that "gathered by the call of God the sisters constitute a monastic church or community" (Const 5).

So in celebrating the feast of the Dedication of the Church, it is our own feast that we are celebrating, the feast of who we are, the feast of who we are becoming: "Like living stones, let yourselves be built into a spiritual house, to be a holy priesthood, to offer spiritual sacrifices acceptable to God through Jesus Christ" (1 Pet 2:5). "Once you were darkness, but now in the Lord you are light. Live as children of light" (Eph 5:8).

We, the church at Tautra, pray in a building with a glass roof. When we are at prayer during these long months of darkness, the roof of our church building is aglow with light. We pray that our presence here among the Norwegian people will be both a witness and a welcome to them: "Come, let us walk in the light of the Lord" (Isa 2:5).

Citizenship Ceremony

Each year, the Norwegian government holds a special ceremony in the various geographical regions for all those who have become new citizens within the year. The 2017 ceremony for the region of North Trondelag, where our monastery is located, was held Saturday, November 11. Some eighty-five new citizens were honored, many of whom had originally come to Norway as refugees, especially from Eritrea. I was happy and proud to be among them.

As I had transferred my stability to Tautra Mariakloster, that is, promised to spend the rest of my life in this community, seeking Norwegian citizenship seemed a logical next step. Like Ruth in the Old Testament, it is to say, "now, these people—both the community and the people of the land—are my people. . . . [here] will I be buried." What the transfer of stability enacted at the community level, the granting of citizenship confirms civilly.

The ceremony was hosted by the fylkesmann (governor). All the new citizens stood and together recited the promise of loyalty to Norway: "As a Norwegian citizen I promise fidelity to Norway, my country, and to the Norwegian society, and I support the democracy and human rights and will respect the laws of the land." Of course we said it in Norwegian, but that is a rough translation. When we practiced this oath before the ceremony, I choked up and almost started crying as the citizenship means so much to me. I love Norway and, as the Norwegians say, *jeg trives her* (I am thriving here). The fylkesmann then presented each new citizen with a lovely book about Norway and citizenship. The mayor of Frosta was also present at the ceremony and presented me with a bouquet of flowers.

I am the third American here to become a Norwegian citizen—actually I have dual citizenship since I am still an American citizen. We have one native Norwegian sister who has been a part of the community from its foundation.

Saint Gertrud the Great: November 16

Truth shining brighter than every light . . . had resolved to temper the thick mist of my darkness. (The Herald of God's Loving Kindness, 2.1.1)[2]

My first encounter with Gertrud was in passing—quite literally in passing. As a young novice, I passed the old life-sized statues of the medieval Benedictine mystics in our monastery hall several times a day. A quick glance told me immediately that these women, depicted with protruding hearts and hearts in hands, were definitely not for me, child of the sixties that I was. So it took me by surprise some twenty years later when a fellow graduate student talked about his research on Gertrud and his reading of Cyprian Vagaggini's discussion of her.[3] He was quite enthused about Gertrud and surprised that I, a monastic woman, neither knew nor cared much about her. He told me that she was a "must read."

Since he was someone I respected a lot, I took him up on it but quickly discovered that she was not an easy read; I was not accustomed to her style and language or to descriptions of visions and accounts of mystical experiences, but I hung in there, and she was definitely well worth the effort. Gertrud became not only a friend, but an inspiration and an example.

[2] *Gertrud the Great of Helfta, The Herald of God's Loving-Kindness, Books 1 and 2*, trans. and annot. Alexandra Barratt, CF 35 (Kalamazoo, MI: Cistercian Publications, 1991), 100.

[3] "The Example of a Mystic: St. Gertrude and Liturgical Spirituality," in Cyprian Vagaggini, *Theological Dimensions of the Liturgy*, trans. Leonard J. Doyle and W. A. Jurgens (1957; Collegeville, MN: Liturgical Press, 1976), 741–803.

She was a learned woman, having been brought up at the monastery of Helfta since the age of four, where she received an excellent education in the liberal arts.[4] As her biographer, a contemporary at Helfta, recounts, she clung "too closely to the liberal arts" and attached "herself too eagerly to the pleasure of human wisdom" for some twenty years, until she had a revelation of the Lord at the age of twenty-five.[5]

Gertrud herself tells of this experience at the beginning of book two.[6] Quite unexpectedly in the dormitory one night, she had a vision of the Risen Lord, recognizable from the wounds in his hand, standing beside her. She heard the words, "I shall free you and I shall deliver you; do not fear." Then the Lord invited her, "return to me at last, and I shall make you drunk with the rushing river of my divine pleasure!" But between them, she says, "there was a hedge of such endless length that I could not see where it ended in front or behind me. On its top the hedge seemed to bristle with such a great mass of thorns that I would never be able to cross it to join [him]. While I stood hesitating because of it . . . he himself seized me swiftly and effortlessly, lifted me up, and set me beside him."[7]

For a month before this vision, Gertrud had experienced what she described as a "storm," a "tempest," which she later understood as the Lord "attempting to pull down the tower of vanity and worldliness into which my pride had grown, even though I bore—an empty boast—the name and habit of the religious life."[8]

---

[4] Gertrud, *Herald* 1.1.1; 2.23.1 (CF 35:37, 162).

[5] Gertrud, *Herald* 1.1.2 (CF 35:38).

[6] Of the five books in the *Herald*, only Book II was written by Gertrud herself. See also Book III, trans. and annot. Alexandra Barratt, CF 63 (Kalamazoo, MI: Cistercian Publications, 1999); Book IV, trans. and annot. Alexandra Barratt, CF 85 (Collegeville, MN: Cistercian Publications, 2018); *The Herald of God's Loving-Kindness, Book V* and *The Book of Special Grace,* CF 86 (Collegeville, MN: Cistercian Publications, 2020).

[7] Gertrud, *Herald* 2.1.2 (CF 35:101).

[8] Gertrud, *Herald* 2.1.1 (CF 35:100–101). See also 2.23.5.

From that time on, after the Risen Lord had lifted Gertrud over the hedge topped with thorns, she says, "calmed by a new joy of the spirit, I began to go forth in the delightful perfume of your balm, so that I too thought easy the yoke and light the burden which a little before I had reckoned unbearable."[9]

Somewhat later she reflects further on the effects of the vision:

> For at that moment you came to me with very clear condescension, in a way both supernatural and pleasurable beyond measure. By a most loving reconciliation you gave me access to knowledge and love of you, and led me into my inmost being which had until then been completely unknown to me. You initiated a relationship with me in supernatural and hidden ways, so that from then on, like friend with friend in his own home, or rather like husband with wife, you were able to take constant pleasure with my soul in my heart.[10]

Gertrud's experience of the Risen Lord—the first of many—led her to place her love of learning subject to—and in the service of—her deep and intimate personal relationship with the Lord, as her biographer recounts:

> No longer a student of literature, then, she became a student of theology and tirelessly ruminated on all the books of the Bible which she could obtain. . . . And in those days she was not sated by the wonderful sweetness and extraordinary pleasure of constant application to divine contemplation or to the careful reading of holy Scripture. To her it seemed honeycomb in the mouth, harmonious music in the ear, and spiritual joy in the heart. Elucidating and clarifying what (others) found obscure, she made compilations from the sayings of the saints . . . and committed to writing many books filled with all sweetness,

---

[9] Gertrud, *Herald* 2.1.2 (CF 35:102).
[10] Gertrud, *Herald* 2.23.5 (CF 35:164–65).

for the general profit of all those who wished to read them. She also composed many prayers . . . and many other examples of spiritual exercises . . . .[11]

The Eucharist was a privileged place of encounter with the Lord for Gertrud and the occasion of many of her mystical experiences.[12] In one case, she recalls,

> after I had received the bread of life and was intent on God and myself, I realized that my soul, like wax carefully softened in the fire, lay on the Lord's breast, as if to be impressed with a seal. Suddenly it seemed to be seized and partially drawn into that treasury [the divine heart] in which the fullness of the divine dwells bodily, and it was sealed with the indelible mark of the bright and ever-tranquil Trinity.[13]

Gertrud's wisdom lives on in her writings, accessible to any who would read them. Our Cistercian Saint Rafael Barón, whose feast day is April 27, spoke of her as one "who loved you [Lord] so much and taught me so much."[14] I will always be grateful to my friend who introduced me to her. At present the cause is being advanced to have her declared a Doctor of the Church. In our day, as in her own, she remains a beacon to the true Light that overcomes all darkness.

---

[11] Gertrud, *Herald*, 1.1.2 (CF 35:39). For Gertrud's spiritual exercises, see, for example, Gertrud the Great of Helfta, *Spiritual Exercises*, trans. Gertrud Jaron Lewis and Jack Lewis, CF 49 (Kalamazoo, MI: Cistercian Publications, 1989).

[12] Olivier Quenardel, "La communion eucharistique dans *Le Héraut de l'Amour Divin* de Sainte Gertrude d'Helfta" (Brepols/Bellefontaine, 1997); Olivier Quenardel, "Conferences on Saint Gertrude of Helfta given at a Session of the Cistercian Monasticate at the Abbey of Himmerod in September 2003," trans. Emmanuel Cazabonne, section 6, para. 2 (http://www.citeaux .net/quenardel/); Ella Johnson, *Eucharistic Theology and Anthropology in the Writings of Gertrude the Great of Helfta*, CS 280 (Collegeville, MN: Cistercian Publications, 2020).

[13] *Herald* 2.7.1 (CF 35:119–20).

[14] M. Rafael Barón, "Life and Writings of Rafael Arnáiz Barón (VII)," trans. Mary Charles Longuemare, CSQ 38, no. 1 (2003): 35–83, here 62.

Thanksgiving: The Fourth Thursday of November

*May God be gracious to us and bless us and make his face
to shine upon us. . . . The earth has yielded its increase;
God, our God, has blessed us. May God continue to bless us;
let all the ends of the earth revere him.* (Ps 67:1, 6-7)

With this Psalm, the responsorial Psalm for the Mass of the
Thanksgiving Day, we begin Lauds or Morning Prayer on
every Sunday and feast day: "Let the peoples praise you,
O God; let all the peoples praise you" (Ps 67:3, 5). Praise is
what the people of God are to be about. Seven times a day, we
gather as a monastic community to sing the praise of God.
Benedict calls these times of prayer, the *Opus Dei*, the work of
God. It is the most important work that we do, and no other
work is to be preferred to it (RB 43.3).

Thanksgiving goes hand in hand with praise. "With gratitude in your hearts sing psalms, hymns, and spiritual songs
to God," Paul exhorts the Colossians. "Whatever you do, in
word or deed . . . do everything in the name of the Lord Jesus,
giving thanks to God the Father through him" (Col 3:16-17).
Thanksgiving goes hand in hand with remembering: "When
you have eaten your fill and have built fine houses and live in
them, and when your herds and flocks have multiplied, and
your silver and gold is multiplied, and all that you have is
multiplied, then do not exalt yourself, forgetting the Lord your
God, who brought you out of the land of Egypt . . ." (Deut
8:12-14). We remember all that God has done for us, whether
as a people, a family, or as an individual person. All that we
have is gift. *All* is from the Lord.

Most nationalities, we discovered, have some type of national celebration of Thanksgiving. Even though we are now
eight different nationalities at Tautra Mariakloster, one thing
that we all have in common culturally is the celebration of a
feast of Thanksgiving. Here at Tautra, we have chosen to celebrate this feast on the fourth Thursday of November, the
American Thanksgiving Day. We were, after all, founded by

an abbey in America, and six of the fourteen of us are American (even though three of the six have become Norwegian citizens).

The day begins as usual with Vigils and Lauds. Our Eucharist (the Greek word means thanksgiving) is a votive Mass of Thanksgiving. That first Eucharist, inaugurated by Jesus the night before he died, was likewise a thanksgiving celebration, a commemoration of the Jewish feast of Passover, a remembrance of what God had done for his people in leading them out of slavery in Egypt into a new life in the Promised Land. It was—and still is today—a festive meal, with traditional food, shared as a family remembering and telling the story of what God had done not only for their ancestors, but for them as well.

At our monastic chapter on Thanksgiving (our daily meeting after Mass and Terce), we remember and share with one another those things for which we are particularly grateful during the past year. For dinner, we have the traditional American Thanksgiving meal of turkey and dressing with all the trimmings, and in the afternoon, those of us who wish can relax together watching a movie. Although the day is about much more than having fun together, it is times like these that unite us together as a monastic family and build up our experience of community.

The celebration of Thanksgiving is an important reminder that we should always "be thankful," as Saint Paul would have it (Col 3:15). As a former novice director once wrote of her experience of life in her later years, "gratitude is the attitude." What a difference an attitude of gratitude can make in our life at any age—especially when the difficulties of life, the disappointments, the negative experiences can loom so large. I once heard a psychologist recommend the daily practice of writing down three things for which one is grateful. It is a good practice, which helps us to focus on the positive and not forget the Lord's blessings. It can lead us into making the prayer of the Psalmist our own: "I give you thanks, O Lord, with my whole heart . . . I sing your praise" (Ps 138:1).

Saint Andrew: November 30

The commandment of the Lord is clear, enlightening the eyes. (Ps 19:8)

The feast of Andrew the apostle falls on the last day of November. In some years, the feast falls in the last week of the church year. In others, it occurs during the first week of Advent. The feast is particularly appropriate for both. While the gospel for the day is taken from Saint Matthew (4:18-22), it is the gospel of John that tells us the most about Andrew. We meet him in the first chapter, a disciple of John the Baptist (1:40).

Earlier in chapter one, the fourth evangelist says of John, the "man sent from God": "He came as a witness to testify to the light, so that all might believe through him. He himself was not the light, but he came to testify to the light. The true light, which enlightens everyone, was coming into the world" (John 1:7-9).

Andrew is one of the two disciples of John the Baptist who were with him when Jesus walked by. Seeing him, John exclaimed, "Look, here is the Lamb of God" (1:36). In the gospel of John, Andrew is named as one of the first two disciples who followed Jesus (John 1:40). The first thing Andrew did when he began following Jesus was to find his brother Peter, to tell him the good news that "We have found the Messiah" and to bring him to Jesus (John 1:41-42).

What a beautiful image to ponder, whether it is the last week of the church year or the first. It is what we are also called to do: to follow Jesus, the true light who has come into the world, and to bring others to him. Andrew ministers in a similar role in chapter twelve, the last mention of him in John's gospel, where he is instrumental in arranging a meeting between Jesus and some Greeks who have come up to Jerusalem for the festival of Passover and who wish to see him (vv. 20-22).

In chapter six of John's gospel, Andrew has a key role in the story of the feeding of the multitude. Sitting on the mountain with his disciples, Jesus looks up and sees the large crowd who have come to listen to him. Where will they get the food needed to feed them? It is Andrew who knows that there is a boy with five barley loaves and two fish in the crowd, but he understandably asks, "what are they among so many people?" (John 6:8-9). In other words, what good is the little that we have? It would never be enough to do what you ask.

Although Andrew is not named again in the chapter, could we not assume that it is he whom Jesus tells to have the crowd sit down and to bring the bread and fish to him? Was Andrew not among those who distributed the bread and fish and gathered up the fragments left over? Here we have another enlightening example given to us who are likewise called to hear the word of the Lord and obey, despite what we consider the meagerness of the resources we have to fulfill it. The Lord's word has power; the Lord's blessing will accomplish it. As today's responsorial Psalm proclaims, and as Andrew no doubt experienced, "The commandment of the Lord is clear, enlightening the eyes" (Ps 19:8).

Finally, Andrew is among those named in the Acts of the Apostles as gathered in prayer in Jerusalem after the Ascension of Jesus, waiting for the fulfillment of the promised Holy Spirit, who will enable them to be witnesses for Jesus not only in Jerusalem, but even "to the ends of the earth" (Acts 1:8).

Andrew is an example for us all, regardless of our state in life. We are all called to be witnesses, sent in the power of the Spirit, to the people and places where we find ourselves each day. Our Cistercian constitutions talk about the "hidden apostolic fruitfulness" of our way of life, which "causes the mystical body of Christ to grow" (Const 7). The word *hidden* refers to the fact that we live within our monastic enclosure and are not engaged in any apostolic activity outside the monastery. Nonetheless, we believe that our prayers of praise and intercession for the needs of all people bear fruit in their lives. We know, from the testimony of many who have called or visited here.

As I mentioned earlier in this chapter, I believe that the very presence of our monastery here in a secular and in many respects non-believing culture must at least provoke thought and questioning in the minds of our many visitors. Why are these women living as they do? How can they be so sure of the existence of God? Many of these visitors tell us of the deep peace they experience in our chapel. No doubt this experience results both from the presence of the Blessed Sacrament in our church and from the positive energy of our prayer and praise. We are delighted to be able to share our monastic prayer with neighbors and friends, with guests and retreatants, with the tourists who come just for one of our times of prayer. May it be a way that we, like Andrew, can tell our brothers and sisters, "We have found the Messiah" (John 1:41).

Christ the King

The Lord is king! Let the earth rejoice; light dawns for the righteous and joy for the upright of heart. (Ps 97:1, 11)

As November draws to a close, the church celebrates the feast of Christ the King on the last, or next to last, Sunday of the month. The liturgical year ends, as it begins, focusing on the Messiah and in particular on this feast, the heavenly exaltation he now enjoys, his coming again in glory as Judge, and his dominion over the whole universe—so the title of today's feast.

Actually the theme of Christ as King is something that permeates the liturgy each and every day. As monastics, we pray the Lord's Prayer ("Thy kingdom come") at the end of six of our liturgical offices each day, in addition to during Mass. God is addressed as King some thirty times in the psalms, and we pray all one hundred and fifty of them in the course of two weeks. The psalms acclaiming God as King are often used during the Christmas season as we celebrate the birth of the Messiah, the anointed royal heir to the throne of David. From the beginning of the monarchy in Israel, the prophets made it clear that God was the king of Israel (1 Sam 8:7). The earthly king was to represent God's care for his people. Not all of Israel's kings succeeded in doing this.

The liturgy's emphasis on God as King is not something I have always recognized. Perhaps that is because as an American the concept of king has always been a bit foreign to me. But now, living in a country that has a royal family has offered me a new perspective, a lived experience of the significance of a king in his country. Although the king is largely a symbolic figure here since Norway is a democracy, he has nonetheless a primary role as the esteemed head of the nation and ruler of the people, as the media coverage of events pertaining to the royal family attests. Particularly impressive is the king's speech to the nation on New Year's Eve, usually an exhortation to the people emphasizing particular values that we as a nation should make our own. Likewise impressive is his solicitous presence with his people during times of tragedy and sorrow, his care and concern for the welfare not only of the Norwegian people, but of all who come to this land regardless of their country of origin or religion. He reminds me of the type of king that the kings of Israel of old were supposed to be.

Today's feast is a celebration of the kingship of Christ, which transcends all other powers: both those on earth and those evil powers of the spiritual world. It is a celebration of the glory Christ now enjoys and to which every believer is destined (Rev 7:9-17). Today's feast anticipates that day when the prayer we pray each day, six times a day, is fulfilled, and God's kingdom will have come; God's will will have been accomplished.

Until that day, we fix our eyes on the heavenly reality that already is. The antiphons and responsories that we sing in the Divine Office are a great help in doing this, particularly as they become ingrained in our minds and hearts through the years. I especially love one response that we sing on this feast with its majestic accompaniment: "His kingdom stands through all

times; the power of his Lordship stands through all generations. Alleluia, alleluia." May it always be so in our minds and
in our hearts.

Anticipating Advent

*"You will do well to be attentive to this [prophetic word] as
to a lamp shining in a dark place, until the day dawns and
the morning star rises in your hearts.* (2 Pet 1:19)

As November's days draw to a close, we always experience
here what I call "Advent sunsets," when the sky becomes
aglow with hues of pinks, blues, and purples. It is magnificent,
like nothing I have ever seen anywhere else, perhaps because
the expanse of sky that we see here is so immense. At the close
of the day, we see glory majestically displayed before our eyes.
Gradually the colors are overshadowed by the approaching
darkness, but we know that the darkness has no lasting power.
It has been—and will be—overcome by light, his light, him
who is the true light, the light of the world (John 8:12). And so
it will be for all eternity. Keep your attention closely fixed on
this prophetic word, focus your attention on the light that
shines in your heart, until that great day when "there will be
no more night . . . for the Lord God will be their light, and
they will reign forever and ever" (Rev 22:5).

December

"The light shines in the darkness . . ."

Sr. Maria Rafael Bartlett, OCSO

Journey

Now
is a season of cold moonlight
and glittering stars, of naked trees, frost
soft on grass at dawn, on copper leaves.
The hills lie low in silence
and the heart feels its days of
woodsmoke and quiet rain, of fire
in the hearth; early darknesses,
unreadable skies
of cloud and calm clarity.

May the waiting,
the living this harsh, stripped season
be blessed.

During the dark season here on the island of Tautra in the Trondheim Fjord in Norway, the phrase *northern light* carries a particular resonance: there is the austerity of winter in a northerly land, and yet also a surprising and distinctive light on bright days. There are vivid sunsets and late dawn skies that appear as comforting winter gift. In the profoundly marked contrast between winter darkness and the special illumination of the season, this Norwegian island is a reflection of life in God with its continual alternations of presence and absence. *Northern light* also conveys something of the inner experience of living in a frontier landscape, a place facing the immensity of God, waiting for dawn and dusk to emerge from beyond the compelling horizon of his mercy.

> *In the tender compassion of our God the dawn from on high*
> *shall break upon us, to shine on those who dwell in darkness*
> *and the shadow of death, and to guide our feet into the way*
> *of peace.* ("Benedictus" at Lauds—Luke 1:79)

Winter on Tautra is a season of contrasts and variation. Days are short, with dawn as late as 9:30 and dusk falling after about 3:00. There can be wild storms with snow and sleet and gale-force winds, the fjord surging with rough water, the color of charcoal under heavy pewter skies. When snow has fallen, there can be days of marvelous stillness and brilliant sunlight magnified by the white ground. Each year, I watch for the first snow to appear on the densely wooded mountains across the water from the monastery. When that first dusting of snow falls there, softening the texture of the mountainsides, the landscape takes on the delicate monochrome appearance of a Chinese brush painting. Often dawn and sunset in winter are spectacular, sky painted in broad strokes of apricot, soft pink, and gold, nature making up for the poverty of such short-lived daylight. In the early morning dark, the cross atop our glass-roofed church projects upwards into the dark sky a shadowed image of itself within the light from the church. Like that imprinted cross, prayer rises, shedding its love within the darkness of the world.

Into our experience of dark interior seasons, there often comes an obscure yet penetrating light, an *inner* illumination that is the source of any unity, compassion, and joy shared here in community—it is the light of the presence of Jesus Christ. This is a light of authentic life, the vibrancy of the true self, and we learn, day by day, to be more present, more permeable to this radiance. That is no easy task. It is the work of grace in us for which we ask, daily. The starkness of a northern winter with its bare trees, the cold, the piercing winds, and barren ground, can be a desert experience for the nun living on Tautra. Yet sometimes the darkness itself can make the brightness of God's frequent gifts to us especially apparent. Sitting in darkness, you cannot fail to notice when a lantern is lit beside you. My own inner life often becomes more sensitive and alive in the winter months here.

The liturgical season of Advent/Christmas is the jewel of our monastic winter. It is inaugurated at Vespers on the eve of the first Sunday of Advent, with the solemn lighting of the first of four candles. These candles mark the weeks of Advent, and the season is characterized too by the use of special Advent music in our liturgy: hymns and antiphons dearly familiar now after my four years as a Cistercian. There are patristic readings during Vigils that speak of the mystery of the incarnation and the coming of the Lord. The themes in our sung communal worship are drawn from the riches of Scripture. As their source, it roots us daily in the word of the Gospel that our life and vocation turn upon. The liturgy reflects the joy and anticipation of this season, in which we celebrate the coming of the Lord into human history, the incarnation.

Last year, our novitiate created an innovative Advent wreath, designing not a wreath at all but a series of four groupings of bamboo-like hollow sticks set a little apart from each other and at different heights, each topped with an Advent candle—three of them the surprising penitential Advent purple, and a soft pink one for the third week before Christmas that is known as "rejoicing" (*Gaudete*) Sunday. The design looked rather Japanese Zen in its style, but the simplicity is all monastic. I found myself moved by the creativity, by the way it conveys a loving impetus in us to express something new and joyful for Advent: "Sing to the Lord a *new* song," Such simple Tautra Advent activities as preparing the wreath, baking Norwegian cookies, singing the seasonal liturgy, decorating our Christmas trees, and rehearsing carols are all celebration. They are also an expression of community. Every moment of our lives has the inexhaustible capacity for a new song within us.

As well as joyful anticipation, Advent carries with it the challenge to deepen a broad perspective of time and eternity, to intensify the personal search to be united with God. It is a tremendous impetus to remember the incomparable glory of that goal that is the foundation of our Christian and monastic vocation: to be united to *God!* Throughout the year, every day we pray the Angelus, entering into Mary's *fiat,* longing for our lives to be surrendered to God as hers was. In Advent, this desire takes on an especially poignant form in our personal and communal worship, and in our ascetic practices, which try to dismantle some of the tyrannical demands of self-centeredness.

Much as I savor the jubilant light of spring and summer here—the unforgettable shimmer of summer days on our island—there is something precious and profoundly interior about the dark season. In a way, it is ideal for contemplative living. When I am deprived of sunlight and the many outdoor enticements one finds on long, warm days, I turn more single-mindedly to my inner priorities. I am less scattered. Our use of candles at our places in the darkened refectory at breakfast and supper times, and the comforting fire blazing in the wood-burner in the refectory in the early mornings, lend the inside of the house a cozy domestic warmth that keeps the bleakness of winter at bay. Darkness often brings astonishing beauty. The dramatic sunsets of early winter can be like explosions of pink and mauve light on the horizon. Cloudless night skies are dense with glittering stars. In winter, the Northern Lights are an unpredictable joy for us. They move as living light across the sky and are always received here with tremendous excitement, with the joy of children experiencing beauty. There might be a handwritten note before Vigils either pinned on the notice board, or set by the kettle in the refectory, announcing *nordlys!* (northern lights!) a modest monastic fanfare alerting us to a display of incomparable beauty outside our windows.

The first time I saw the Northern Lights was after Compline during my first year of formation, on the eve of the feast of the Immaculate Conception, December 8. As we emerged from the church and were hanging up our cloaks or cowls, a sister came and beckoned me to follow her to the immense walls of glass in our cloister where some others were standing gazing out. My heart leapt: could it be the Northern Lights? I'd seen photographs in books, but nothing could have prepared me for the reality: we are simply *familiar* with what we will see in the sky. Stars, a full moon, shifting clouds lit up by the moonlight—all beautiful, and familiar. In spite of dry scientific explanations of the phenomenon of the aurora borealis, to see light alive and moving in a dark sky is a breathtaking experience. I find in the Northern Lights a deeply spiritual quality. The living light is an image for me of God's presence, and each time I see it, I hold it to myself with gratitude as a gift from him. It is a sinuous dance of the Holy Spirit. Like God's manifestations in our daily lives, the lights in the sky are always different. Some funnel upwards like towering spotlights, then sway from side to side like a searchlight. There can be pale green soft light, an iridescence that moves across the entire sky like a curtain opening. Sometimes it is subtle white light just gently shifting in the immense sky as you crane your neck to take it all in. When there has been a dramatic display here, the whole community has gathered spontaneously outside on the grass behind our monastery, each of us standing with head turned upwards, each of us exclaiming in wonder. It is more beautiful, more a gift, because it appears at night. "The heavens declare the glory of God and the firmament shows forth the work of his hands" (Ps 18:2). For me, the Northern Lights cry out this night word: "I am alive within your deepest darkness."

Because of the temperate nature of the Gulf Stream in the fjord, we actually get very little snow here on Tautra. This was a surprise to me, expecting the whole of Norway to be snow-bound all winter. Our snow, even when quite heavy, rarely lasts more than a few days. But the snow here brings a soft white light and a wonderful hush that subtly alters the feel of the house, illuminating the interior on grim dark days, falling softly like a whisper, a pure, winter gift.

The snow entices some of us to play in it during our meridian rest time. Several of us exult like children, flying down our hill towards the iconic boathouse on the shore, on Norwegian kick-sleds called *sparks*. One sister loves to traverse the snowy island fields on cross-country skis. When it snows, the morning work of the more energetic and physically robust of us begins with the invigorating labor of clearing paths around the monastery. When a heavy snow begins to melt, there is a remarkable sound in our church of ice and snow sliding from the glass roof, tumbling with a thud to the ground.

Being on an island, we are buffeted in winter by some dramatic storms with winds so forceful that the stony shore can be completely re-shaped by the fierce waves. I remember the first time I experienced one of these storms here. It was Compline, and the wall of glass behind the altar in church was bearing the brunt of the gale. The evening was black behind the glass, and I could hear a disconcerting sound as if the glass was buckling. I visualized the entire wall of glass shattering and imploding on us; I felt anxious and unsafe. The wail and attack of the wind accompanied us through the night, and I had to trust that the house would stand firm. By morning, my anxiety had lessened: we had survived unscathed. I then learned that the glass of which so much of the monastery is made is actually designed to bend in high winds. That is a remarkable lesson for me in withstanding turbulence inside myself. I need to let my faith help me to bend, to be supple in storm and gale. It is our *faith* that designs us for this resilience.

In Advent an asceticism marks the weeks as a time of special preparation for a sacred season. We are encouraged to narrow our focus more single-mindedly to God and to surrender to his work within us. For Cistercians, this spiritual exercise does not take the form of extraordinary external practices but is a real labor to pray with greater vigilance, to spend longer with spiritual reading, to cut back on personal correspondence, to work again with being more silent, to forgive one another more readily, to welcome joy into oppressed areas of our hearts. This is to "make straight the way of the Lord," in Isaiah's words used to describe the call of John the Baptist. In his vocation as one who clears a direct path for the coming God, John plays a strong role in our monastic life. Daily in the *Benedictus*, we remember his prophetic message and his role in preparing the human heart for Jesus: "And you, child, shall be called the prophet of the Most High. You shall go before him to prepare his way" (Luke 1:76). In this time of preparation for Christmas, John strides onto center stage in the third Sunday of Advent in the gospel reading, and through his commanding presence we are urged to a conversion that brings genuine transformation. In this vital season of the church's life, we concentrate on conversion with heightened intensity. For those with a monastic vocation, such work brings joy with it. The ascetic effort is work that strives to develop a cleansed and spacious inner life that is turned towards God like the face of an eager child. The expression on the face of such a child is one of love and trust.

The rhythm of the liturgical seasons ripens in us a growing appreciation of all that God has done for us in Jesus. That growth is another element that never ends if we surrender to all the prompts that our monastic life offers us daily. In Advent and during the celebration of the Christmas season, our gaze zooms in as if through a magnifying glass on the mystery of the incarnation, perceived every year with deeper clarity and deeper love. These depths are immeasurable. Our immersion into the spiritual truth of the mystery of the incarnation ultimately widens out from this single theme because all moments of the life of Jesus are profoundly, irrevocably interwoven. When I contemplate the birth of Jesus, I am implicitly contemplating the death of the One who was born and the resurrection of the child who was given to us. These strands are continually interwoven into the whole, seamless fabric of salvation.

My personal experience of prayer tends to be what is called dark or obscure prayer, often painfully arid, without words and images. In the dark season of winter, somehow I discover a satisfying congruence between outside and inside. My prayer of naked being before God somehow feels more natural, and I am more easily at home in it than at other times. "If I say: 'Let the darkness hide me and the light around me be night,' even darkness is not dark for you, and the night is as clear as the day" (Ps 138:11-12).

From late spring to the end of autumn, the trees behind our monastery, seen from the refectory, comprise a lush leafy screen between us and the fjord. In winter, bare trees enable us to see through to a wider expanse of the water. For me, there is a parallel there with conditions for contemplation in winter. I once read a book called *The Light Inside the Dark*, and I love to return to that image that is so fundamentally Christian: "The light shines in the darkness and the darkness can never extinguish it" (Prologue to John's gospel). The light deep inside the chaos of our anguished world is Jesus and his message of God's merciful love. The light is hope, faith's fruit; a candle held resolutely in the cold storm of night. It is love, received and believed in, come what may.

Lectio Divina

> Rain streams down
> on windows that hold
> against the winter night.
>
> Brittle plants shiver,
> unprotected
> under a cold dense darkness.
>
> On the desk,
> In lamplight,
> Scriptures lie open,
> And I read.

The Word, this
new December morning,
like the mothering dawn
extinguishes the night.

Advent asks us, every year, to wake up: "Now is the time for us to wake from sleep" (Rom 13:11). The winter season here on Tautra gives a special impetus to this demand. When I pray in the dark church after Vigils, sometimes the darkness lulls me back towards sleep, and if my prayer is especially empty, I am tempted by compelling thoughts of my warm bed, attracted by the hibernation of sleep when the world outside is so dark and cold. There's a parallel here for all the year. As Christians, we are called to be utterly awake in a benighted world in order to use that vigilance as compassion, to resist being asleep to the almost overwhelming need of the world in its distress. Being fully awake is the soul work of a lifetime. It pulls us continually to a wrenching self-knowledge from which humility can eventually be formed. We can never entirely fulfill our personal vocation if we do not do the work of casting off sleep. I have only to attempt to eat my breakfast mindfully, to discover that after two mouthfuls of bread, my mind has traveled long miles, and I am chasing yesterday's resentments, worried about today's work, reliving dreams from the night before. The practice of remaining inside the experience of the taste and texture of the bread, the silence of the refectory, the flickering candle on the table in winter, the thirst for a cup of tea, has a resonance for staying in the truth of the heart at every moment, acknowledging my poverty, my constant need for God. Every attempt to practice mindfulness is a sharp lesson for me, revealing how asleep I often am to the life of my own heart, and thus to God.

When we look at photographs of the universe, we experience an awe at the incomprehensible immensity and mystery of the galaxies, in which our planet is a speck of dust. We need to let that same kind of perspective deepen in us when we contemplate the real existence of God. Most often, I experience the immensity of God and smallness of myself through nature, as when gazing up at the night sky full of stars, or in a graced silent prayer when my nothingness calmly finds peace in God's All. Sometimes, in the darkness of a winter Compline, I suddenly pray, "God!" with a surge of sudden astonished joy at the real existence of God. In those moments, I am vibrantly, gratefully awake. "In his temple, they all cry 'Glory!'" (Ps 29:9).

In Advent, as I walk from the refectory along the stone-floored cloister to the church, I pass our smooth white statue of a young, seated Mary with the small child Jesus a naked toddler standing close beside her. It reflects the tremendous fact that at the incarnation, God became a real human being. In our statue, Jesus is a normal little boy, his legs bent casually so that he leans informally, with an intimate familiarity, against his mother's skirts. He is not portrayed as a haloed figure of precocious wisdom but as a real child. His nakedness reveals his vulnerability and his proximity to an innocent babyhood. With the fertile fire of his own Spirit, God ignited a new life within the Virgin's womb: *God himself* entered into her womb. Who could have imagined that the all-powerful God would accomplish so intimate an entry into human life? With that instant, the world and what it means to be human changed forever. Yet human consent was a necessary part of this divine initiative. To be like Mary in her example of perfect discipleship, we must attend to our own responsibility in how we respond to the transforming touch of God's love.

The seventeenth-century Carmelite Saint John of the Cross wrote a small poem for Advent that says, translated from Spanish, "The Virgin, heavy with child, is coming down the road. Who will shelter her?" I love these simple lines, with their startling paradox of a "Virgin" being "heavy with child." She seems to me a lonely figure walking towards us, and I want to cry out "*I* will shelter you!" But the truth is, so often there is no room at the inn. I pray for a more spacious heart so that

I will have the capacity to give her the sheltering hospitality of a purified love. Her own love made a space of immeasurable proportions: "Be it done unto me according to your word" (Luke 1:38). What a response from an undivided heart! And its consequence? "And she conceived by the Holy Spirit."

Pure and trusting love alone made the birth of Jesus possible. Mary doesn't need a palace or even a well-appointed inn if she is to give birth to Jesus again in us: she was happy to bear Jesus in the rough poverty of a stable, filled with animal smells. That stable or rough-hewn cave is what we are like inside. It's enough. She looks at this poor ground of our hearts and sees only the space of the welcome she needs as shelter for the intimate act of birth. At Tautra Mariakloster, our name proclaims the honored place Mary has in our life. As the perfect disciple of Jesus and as our loved mother, we turn to her throughout our days, singing her praise at the end of every Office. In this way, we not only cherish her but remember our call to be whole like her in our faith and our love. The last word on our lips each evening is "Maria."

Saint Paul speaks of how the "whole of creation is groaning in one great act of giving birth" (Rom 8:22). With a particular poignancy in Advent, this scriptural image applies to our individual lives too, as we yearn for the coming of Emmanuel, of God-with-us. Our careless familiarity with the physical reality of childbirth can cause us to stop perceiving how miraculous it is. If we imagine seeing, for the first time as adults, a woman in full-term pregnancy, how astonishing to discover the capacity of a woman's body to stretch so enormously to accommodate the growing child inside. We are capable of a similar but *greater* suppleness in our spiritual lives as we learn to make space for God and, through grace, to expand as he begins to fill us with himself. We will never have enough of God inside us; we always have capacity for deeper union. In its intense longing, Advent embraces both the coming of the Lord in the incarnation and how we ourselves interiorize that birth, and also the second, consummating coming of Jesus in glory. Saint Bernard wrote of a triple coming: in essence, Jesus *came* into human life, he *comes* to us now in every moment, he *will come* again at the end of time. These comings are held together in a profound unity. Our longing is not for our personal fulfillment alone but for the final fulfillment of a universal salvation.

In Norway, the landscape reflects our monastic journey in many ways. I relish living in a country where there are distinct seasons. Our lives, both inner and outer, are marked by seasons, rhythms of darkness and light, growth and fallowness. Our glass-roofed church with its wall of glass behind the altar keeps us close to the outside world. We are enclosed yet never cut off. In spring, we see and hear raucous seagulls on the roof; other birds cast darting shadows as they fly swiftly across; sunlight and moonlight both reflect a lattice-work pattern on our pale wood walls and stone floor. Raindrops glisten in long pearl-like strands on the wall of glass behind the altar in the church, in cloister and refectory. Our monastery was built to include a number of inner gardens, open spaces that bring the landscape inside. Alongside the choir area of the church is a small garden with a tall evergreen tree, and in winter there are always some sturdy green plants thriving, sometimes softened by snow.

The skies here are constantly changing, from moment to moment: a forbidding gray or a luminous, pastel blue, ragged clouds torn by wind, billowing rounded clouds rising like smoke behind the mountains across the fjord, sculpted clouds suspended in an ocean of sky like islands. Our awareness of the water also punctuates our day, a backdrop to our prayer and work. We eat facing the fjord with its bird life and passing boats, and we gaze at the water from church, so we are attuned to its tremendous variations in color and mood through the seasons. On an island, we often experience what seem to be several seasons in a single day. My own inner life can be just like that, and it reassures me to see those fluctuations reflected in nature. Last winter, I became fascinated with the shape of bare trees, noticing the bold upward-reaching geometry of the branches, as if the roots had been turned up to face the sky. They image for me a stark longing, a deep need that I direct towards the Lord and that I am aware of when all foliage and fruit is stripped away. To be aware of this aching need is to know oneself awake, even if only for an interlude. I find the sight of the naked, beseeching winter trees an echo of my own nature: companions for a desert journey.

Learning to Wait

Advent comes at a time when we feel the dark palpably close in around us each day, and in this experience there are images of both womb and waiting, a new surrender in the obscurity of faith. Waiting is a prominent discipline of Advent, and learning to wait is vital. It is a way of learning to live contentedly with the pain of a certain kind of profound desire that is so deeply a part of relationship with God. When candidates are discerning whether they may be called here to Tautra, there is always a concern regarding how the dark season will affect people. Some are vulnerable to depression in a time of prolonged darkness. As is evident in what I am writing, I love the Tautra winter, but it lasts much longer than the English winter I'm used to. Observable green and flowering spring does not arrive here until May. By March, I am longing fiercely, almost resentfully, for the first signs of buds and leaves, weary of bare branches and a lack of rich green. It is no bad thing to stay with this feeling of longing. It relates directly to strengthening my faith. The days here are short in winter, the night's darkness long, with sunrise delayed until nearly 10 a.m., but inexorably the new dawn does come, each morning. Its coming is a gift, like touches of God in our lives when all looks set to remain dark, like the fecundity of spring after the winter.

In winter, the darkness and the gloom of rainy days, storms, the churning fjord crashing in high winds against what I call lighthouse point, the suddenness of a transitory radiance, illuminating the tops of naked trees, then disappearing back to grey—these all have a wild quality that stimulates my interior life in this season. In winter when we rise before 4 a.m., the lighthouse can be seen from our refectory, blinking its reassuring Morse code like a word from God, rhythmic as a heartbeat: "Here I am in the dark. I am here all night, so you don't founder on the rocks. Here I am." Our monastic community too works as a beacon for others who are lost in a wild darkness. In our shared life here we experience God's guiding presence, and an essential part of our vocation is to witness to the possibility of intimacy with God. Norway is not a Catholic country, and in spite of officially being Lutheran, like much of the Western world it can barely be called Christian anymore, so widespread is a lack of faith. Many people visit our community, sometimes simply coming to see the church after being in our small shop, and we have many retreatants and visitors who tell us the impact it makes on them to see a group of people enacting together their faith in God. This enables our life to begin to burn away the toxic smog of an ever-encroaching consumerism and secularism, creating a patch of clear sky where people can breathe a wholesome air, and just be, in silence.

> Cold salt tides swell and retreat;
> long sparkling days fall into twilight and the shuttered
> nights of deeper dark. And when the winter comes,
>   and the dark
> folds in around us like a shroud, when
> even the mountains are lost,
> there is a fire burning in the hearth.
> Lives given and consumed like dry wood, in a silence
> that streams to its source.
> Church, cloister, cell, heart—in darkness
> alight with the Word.
> From buffeted night, Christ rises.
> In midnight's destitution, he comes
> wild and tender; broken and whole.
> He is
> our redeeming dawn.

"O come, O come, Emmanuel."

In the days approaching Christmas, we find at the back of our church or surreptitiously delivered into our kitchen generous domestic gifts of baked goods, flowers, sweets, and fruits from many of our neighbors and friends. It's quite overwhelming to just receive this bounty, given, as God's love is given, utterly gratuitously. It creates powerful bonds of community, of kinship, and it underlines the special quality of Christmas. Two close friends of the community, a married couple, bring us three magnificent Christmas trees every year, and we share coffee and cake with them in gratitude. The day they bring the trees means it's almost Christmas. We don't decorate the trees until just before Christmas Eve, and we form small teams, each choosing its own way to embellish the beautiful trees from our old stock of ornaments. There is always a towering tree in the cloister, with that astringent scent permeating the space, and I still feel a childlike pleasure when the tree's colored lights are switched on for the first time. Christmas!

In our liturgy, as we reach the final week before Christmas, our worship reflects a heightened intimacy with God in the form of the well-known O antiphons. This is a series of antiphons that preface the Magnificat at Vespers, and each begins with a sung O, prolonged, a soaring and dipping melody in monastic chant. The O sings of our deep desire and our praise for the God who is to come, and who has already come. Each antiphon is a prayer to an aspect of Christ, using ancient Scriptural imagery, rich in associations for the Christian: "O Immanuel," "O Dayspring," "O root of Jesse". . . . The ancient O antiphons express a rich theology and the deep longing so central to Advent.

For the last couple of years, we have explored the riches of these O antiphons together in our chapter meetings, finding ways to express for one another what associations and meanings they have for us. One of our novices created a vivid way to express "O Emmanuel," designing a musical notation put up on the wall. The notes were of the actual Emmanuel anti-phon, but each member of community was represented by a note, so that the whole form conveyed the melody and harmony of our relationships to one another in singing our longing for this God who is "with us." There is a powerful truth there about community and about communal worship, about how the community comprises a whole in which relationships create a harmonious life.

> *And the Word was made flesh and dwelt amongst us.*
> (Prologue, John's gospel)

At last, after the weeks of preparation and longing, the eve of the celebration of the incarnation arrives. On Christmas Eve, we celebrate Midnight Mass, attended usually by a small number of visitors. It is the climactic moment of our worship in this season, and it begins with us moving out of choir, standing just in front of our guests to sing several Christmas carols. This simple element marks the celebration as something special to us and presents it with love to our guests to share in. As Mass begins, when the bells ring out their *Gloria in excelsis Deo* in a double peal, it is like the rejoicing word after long ruminative silence. *And the Word became flesh and dwelt amongst us.* It is irrepressible joy breaking out, the sound almost bursting through the glass roof.

As our community has grown into an international group, we have had intercessions in several different languages at our Christmas Midnight Mass. Then at the end of the service, all join around the altar, near the crib, and we sing *Silent Night* in Norwegian and English. After this special Mass, the community and any visitors, guests, and volunteers move together into our scriptorium, which is transformed into a modest banquet hall for the occasion. We light candles on the long tables, and one large table has a festive array of food set out, with coffee and hot spiced punch. Much of the food is contributed by guests; it is a welcome feast at an hour when we would normally be in bed.

After the midnight Eucharist, the peace at the heart of the celebration is strongly felt and shared with one another. It is good that friends are embraced within the monastic enclosure at this special time. For us, the festivity comes at the end of a long day of activity and prayer, a day busy with food preparation and liturgical rehearsal. The joyful atmosphere of friendship and festivity somehow manages to overcome our fatigue. We talk, eat, and laugh together, exchanging heartfelt "Happy Christmas" greetings (*God jul!*) now that Christmas Day has arrived. "Joy to the world! The Lord is come."

> *Now, Master, you can let your servant go in peace, just as you promised; because my eyes have seen the salvation which you prepared for all the nations.* (Luke 2:29-30)

And the Word was made flesh, and dwelt amongst us. When I consider the eschatological waiting of Advent and the Christmas season, those words from the Prologue to John's gospel are my food. They are a word that hums, resounds throughout the sacred season. Our God came, and in such an unimaginable way, to his faithful Anawim: he will not fail to complete his work of love.